THE
ONE DIRECTION
STORY

AN UNAUTHORIZED BIOGRAPHY

D1023724

THE
ONE DIRECTION
STORY

AN UNAUTHORIZED BIOGRAPHY

DANNY WHITE

First edition for the United States published in 2012
by Barron's Educational Series, Inc.

First published in Great Britain in 2012 by
Michael O'Mara Books Limited,
9 Lion Yard, Tremadoc Road,
London SW4 7NQ
www.mombooks.com

All inquiries should be addressed to:
Barron's Educational Series, Inc.
250 Wireless Boulevard
Hauppauge, NY 11788
www.barronseduc.com

ISBN-13: 978-1-4380-0247-7

Library of Congress Control No.: 2012942863

Date of Manufacture: October 2012
Manufactured by: B12V12G, Berryville, VA

Printed in the United States of America

9 8 7 6 5 4 3 2

CONTENTS

INTRODUCTION

A month can be a long and eventful time in pop music—just ask One Direction. For Liam, Louis, Niall, Harry, and Zayn, the thirty days of April 2012 were packed with international incident and intrigue, terrific triumphs, and turbulent torment. Just two years prior, they were five ordinary teenage boys, counting the days before they auditioned as solo artists on *The X Factor*. Their lives have been anything but ordinary ever since.

During April, they were invited to the White House by Michelle Obama. They announced—and then sold out in record time—a headline concert at America's most prestigious concert venue, Madison Square Garden. They entered the studio to record with the Canadian prince of pop, Justin Bieber. As the United States fell in love with the band, they appeared on the American entertainment television programs *The Today Show* and *Saturday Night Live*. Meanwhile, a shadow was cast over their American dream as they faced a lawsuit from a U.S. band of the same name. Members of the American band soon received death threats from furious fans of their British namesakes.

As April continued, the band jetted to the southern hemisphere. There, they were delighted to discover that Australian and New Zealander girls were just as devoted to them as their American and British counterparts. The band was mobbed by an army of fans in Sydney and, on one occasion, a young man with no connection to the band was surrounded by screaming fans in a moment of mistaken identity. As security tightened, one Australian fan said she would be willing to risk being shot to get close to them. Then, a slice of toast, half-eaten by band member Niall, went to auction. It attracted bids of nearly $160,000.

While celebrating the news that their debut single sold over one million copies in America, each band member pocketed a reported $3.1 million. Louis decided that he wanted to buy a pet monkey. As if all this wasn't enough for one month, they were simultaneously flattered and deflated when they were praised by pop princess Rihanna and then told that Madonna had announced that she doesn't know who they are. Before the month was over, the band also met some koalas, and then went surfing in the Pacific Ocean. There was still time for Niall to contract food poisoning and for two other members to take part in a 630-foot (192-m) bungee jump. Then, they arrived back in Britain and were greeted by thousands of screaming fans.

No wonder the frenzy that surrounds One Direction has been compared to "Beatlemania." Their popularity is simply immense however you measure it. They are the first U.K. pop group to debut at number one on the American album chart. The same album went straight to number one in Britain and twelve other countries. They have over 12 million followers on Twitter and 3.6 million on Facebook. They have amassed over 204 million YouTube views. A Google spokesperson has revealed that 3.35 million people are typing One Direction related phrases into the search engine each month.

One Direction is Britain's—and arguably the world's—most popular boy band. How they rose to the top is a fascinating and inspiring story.

1 HARRY STYLES

When the five members of One Direction finally get a chance to stop working for a moment, take a break, and survey the success they have made of their pop careers, none will be as calm and unruffled as Harry Styles. Harry's lovable, nonchalant persona is not a contrived attempt at achieving an image of "pop cool." He really is, at heart, a laid-back guy. His detachment has been tested, too: life had thrown him some curve balls in the years before he became famous, but he played them all with a cool, straight bat, rarely breaking a sweat.

When Harry's mom, Anne Cox, stops to think about her son's fame and his many professional achievements, she finds it difficult to wrap her head around it. To the outside world, he might be the hearthrob from One Direction—a young man known in many countries and endlessly discussed by both his fans and the mainstream media—but to his mom, he will always be something else as well: "At the end of the day, he's my little baby and there he is on stage in front of millions of people," she said.

Anne's little baby was born on February 1, 1994. He was her second child—she already had a daughter named Gemma. Anne was just as thrilled when she became a mother the second time around. She named her precious son Harry Edward. No one knew it then, but a star had just been born.

Harry's early years were spent in Cheshire, in the northwest of England. It is an area of lush, rural beauty surrounding a number of upscale towns and villages. Holmes Chapel, one of those villages, is where Harry spent much of his childhood. It is a comfortable neighborhood with basic amenities, including easy access to public transportation for those who want to hit up Manchester for something wilder. Cheshire itself is not an area with a massively famous artistic heritage, though indie rockers Ian Curtis and Tim Burgess both come from there. When Harry auditioned for *The X Factor*, he described the area as "quite boring—nothing much happens there," though on a more admiring note he admitted, with a smile, that it is "picturesque." He is now one of Cheshire's most famous sons.

As Harry became a toddler, he was sent to a nursery school called Happy Days. Harry feels it is an appropriately named institution because he had so many enjoyable times there. It was a small establishment so he was never short of attention and care. He was a well-behaved boy who enjoyed playing with toys and participating in games. Harry has always been fun-loving, but he's creative, too. He began to show his artistic side at home at the breakfast table, where he would draw on his toast with food coloring before he ate it. He was always encouraged to express himself—a key factor in the development of any budding artist. In time, he learned to juggle and tried his hand at learning some musical instruments. Always funny and entertaining, Harry was becoming an all-around performer. "He's always loved attention and making people laugh," Anne told *Now* magazine. "He's certainly not shy about himself. Ever since he was young he's made people smile. I always thought he'd end up on the stage."

When he was seven, Harry's life, which had been

generally very happy and enjoyable until then, took a darker turn when his parents told him that they were getting divorced. His first reaction to this bombshell was to burst into tears. He loves both his parents, so he hated to think of them going their separate ways. At this age, Harry was old enough to understand the pain caused by the separation, but not yet old enough to understand or control his own reaction to the pain. Children of that age who face such a testing upheaval typically go through feelings of grief, shame, resentment, confusion, and even anger as they come to terms with the situation.

Though Harry has always put an upbeat spin on his reaction to the divorce in public, it definitely hurt him, and—to some extent—influenced the course of his life since the split. He says that he bounced back fairly quickly and learned to live with the situation. As he has confirmed since, as a seven-year-old he did not— and *could* not—fully grasp what was going on in his parents' minds. There were many practical changes for him to come to terms with. After the divorce he and his sister moved into a new house with their mom, settling in a more rural part of Cheshire. They lived above a pub where Anne became the landlady. There were lots of changes going on in his life, but Harry managed to roll with the punches. He made a new friend, a boy named Reg who was a little older than him, and got to know the new area. He discovered a dairy farm where they made delicious ice cream a few miles from his new home. He loved the ice cream, and life always felt good when he had some after biking down the road.

Despite his parents' divorce, Harry remained full of energy and enthusiasm. Rather than truly misbehaving—he only got into one fight throughout his school years—he channeled his drive into hard work. He particularly enjoyed English and RE (Religious Education) classes. In English, he was good at expressing himself on the page and often achieved good grades for his essays. An extrovert at heart, he also looked forward to drama classes, and it was through these that he made his singing debut. "The first time I sang publicly was in a school production—the rush that I got was something that I really enjoyed and wanted to do more of," he said. That rush was the feeling of his love of performing and being in the spotlight. The plays that Harry appeared in include *Chitty Chitty Bang Bang*, in which Harry played the part of Buzz Lightyear. Although Buzz Lightyear, originally from *Toy Story*, is not a traditional part of *Chitty Chitty Bang Bang*, the school was able to break away from tradition with their version of the play. As an Aquarius (his astrological sign), Harry has always been comfortable with experimentation so this was fine by him. On another occasion, he played the title role in a play about a mouse named Barney.

In addition to acting, Harry was also encouraged to sing. It was his father who first sparked his interest in music. As it became clear that Harry loved to sing, his grandfather bought him a karaoke machine and one of the first songs that Harry crooned along to was Elvis Presley's "Girl of My Best Friend."

While attending the Holmes Chapel Comprehensive School, Harry stumbled upon an exciting way of further fulfilling his desire to perform in front of an audience—he was invited to join a rock band. A friend of his named Will was looking for a lead vocalist for a band he was putting together. He asked Harry to come along and practice with the band. All the members were very happy with handsome Harry as their front man, and the band's line-up was complete. Then they just needed to agree on a name for themselves. It was Harry who suggested the random name White Eskimo. It is a strange moniker—sounding more like a nightclub or a cocktail than a teenage rock band. Nevertheless, it was certainly distinctive and nobody had any better ideas, so they went with it. Harry has an inventive mind: This would not be the last time that he came up with a band name.

White Eskimo was influenced by punk-pop acts such as Californian band Blink-182. Harry is also a fan of Jack's Mannequin and other similar artists. However, three of his biggest musical inspirations stood entirely outside the punk-pop genre: Michael Jackson, Elvis Presley, and Freddie Mercury. One of the songs he loved during his childhood was "Free Fallin" by John Mayer, and he also had a soft spot for Michael Bublé's music. Each member of White Eskimo had his own influences—and together they made a fairly decent band.

Soon, they played at school events and weddings. The first song that White Eskimo performed live was Bryan Adam's "Summer of '69." Then, the band noticed there was a local talent show being held for groups. They decided to enter it. As Harry later explained to *X Factor* host Dermot O'Leary, "We entered a 'Battle of the Bands' competition about a year and a half ago and we won. Winning Battle of the Bands and playing in front of that many people really showed me that's what I wanted to do. I got such a thrill when I was in front of people singing, it made me want to do more and more."

The victory made an impression on Harry's school principal, Denis Oliver, who attended the competition, held in the school cafeteria. Mr. Oliver remembered later, "White Eskimo won the Battle of the Bands here when he [Harry] was in Year 10. He's performed in a lot of assemblies." Harry's singing had clearly made quite an impact on his first live audiences.

Even some of the kids who were at the shows remember what they saw. Bethany Lysycia told the *Crewe Chronicle*, "They were really good. Everyone was really impressed, especially with Harry. We all knew he could sing because we would see him singing in the corridors all the time. He was always going to be a star and I think he's getting better and better."

Videos have been published on the Internet of

the band performing "Summer of '69" at a wedding. Although Harry's voice is, naturally, quite a lot higher in these videos than it is now, he cuts a familiar figure on the stage: He bounces, looks down at the floor as he takes deep breaths, and generally comes across as the same guy who is now in One Direction. Another song that they played regularly was "Be My Girl" by the band Jet.

Their wedding performance earned them their first paycheck. The band was paid $250 for the show. They split it evenly among them, so each band member got about $62. As Harry fondly remembered, they were also offered free sandwiches. However, more valuable than the money and the sandwiches combined was the experience and the feedback. People were telling him that he was a natural singer and front man. His charisma and stage presence were so impressive that one of the guests at the wedding, a music producer, compared him with one of British music history's finest front men, Mick Jagger of the Rolling Stones. What an honor—Harry felt so proud and excited by all the positive feedback he received. He was becoming a mini local celebrity and heartthrob long before he became nationally, and then internationally, famous. That fact, together with his boyish good looks and charm, meant he was getting plenty of attention from girls long before he shot to national fame through *The X Factor*.

Harry remembers a friend he had when he was six as his first close female friend. She was the daughter of a friend of Anne's and the two were very sweet together. Harry even bought them matching teddy bears. He describes her as "the cutest little girl." When he was twelve, he had his first girlfriend, and he has stated that his first kiss was with a girl from his school.

A girl named Lydia Cole told the *Crewe Chronicle* that Harry had been her first boyfriend. "What you see on screen is what you get" she said. "That's Harry—he's always been charming and cheeky." Rumors that circulated about Harry once he became famous portray him as very experienced with girls and very quick to show off his prowess. "Harry was bragging about how many girls he'd dated," an "insider" quoted by *Now* magazine claimed. "Harry's very flirty." Of all the members of 1D, it was Harry who seemed most comfortable when dealing with attractive female personalities during their time on *The X Factor* and beyond. The legacy of his past experience was visible in the smooth, confident, and assured persona he took when speaking with them.

As for his family, it got a new member when his mother met his stepdad, Robin. The couple had been careful to consider Harry and Gemma's feelings by introducing their partnership gradually and carefully. Harry thought Robin was great and was elated—if a bit amused—to learn that he had proposed to Anne while they sat watching the soap opera *Coronation Street.*

Other memories from his childhood include the time he ate way too much food at a TGI Fridays restaurant and vomited all over his sister Gemma on the way home. His love of food never caused weight issues for Harry, partly because he loves sports, with badminton, football, and cricket being three of the games that he enjoyed playing. He also became a feared opponent at the bowling alley. Unsurprisingly, one of his favorite classes at school was gym. He began to represent the local soccer team, often playing as goalie.

He got himself a part-time job working at a local business, the W. Mandeville Bakery. His boss, Simon Wakefield, told the BBC that Harry had been a model employee. "He used to clean the floor at night and work on a Saturday, serving customers in the shop. He was great, he was good to have around—there was always a good atmosphere when he was about." Harry's former boss also said he "was really popular with the customers when he used to work the counter." One can imagine his charisma and good looks being a hit with the customers.

Harry was ready to transfer his natural charm onto the national stage. Like millions of other Brits, he loved to watch television talent shows, including *The X Factor*. When he saw young contestants succeed on that series, he began to believe that he too stood a chance of doing so. To use a phrase that would become apposite for him in the future, he "dared to dream." Local talent shows and weddings were all well and good, but to audition in front of the fearsomely respected Simon Cowell and his fellow judges, as well as millions of television viewers, was an entirely different prospect. So he grabbed an application form, which his mom filled out for him, and sent it in. From there, it was just a matter of counting down the days to his audition. He told his bandmates what he planned to do and they had no hard feelings. The bass guitarist Nick Clough said, "We're happy for him and wish him all the best." The lead guitarist, Haydn Morris said, "Everyone here at school is behind him. It's great."

Fired up with ambition and hope, Harry was open-minded about his life plans in the years ahead as he approached his *X Factor* audition. All he knew was that whatever he ended up doing as a job, he would want it to be something he could earn a good living from. He did not want to struggle financially as an adult. He had plans to go to college and study Law, Business, and Sociology. In his spare time he worked at the bakery. As you will see, some of the other boys who ended up in One Direction arrived to audition very emotionally on edge. They felt their very future was hanging on getting a "yes" from the judges. Blasé Harry was eager to succeed, but was less uptight about the outcome. For him, the experience was more about discovery—he wanted to know if he had it in him to become a professional singer. If the answer turned out to be negative, that was fine by him, but at the very least he'd give it a shot.

Sometimes, when someone has a dream in life, they find a reason not to pursue it. Rather than focusing on all the things that could go right, they imagine things that could go wrong. Harry's example shows that at times, it is worth taking the more positive approach of simply pausing to consider whether one has anything to lose by taking a chance. He did not approach *The X Factor* with a fear that his life depended on success. He just decided to try it out to see what would happen. Life is full of choices—young Harry Styles had just made a very wise one.

2 LOUIS TOMLINSON

Louis is the dark horse of the band. Unlike Harry, Liam, and Niall, and even Zayn to an extent, he went virtually unnoticed during the early phases of *The X Factor*. Few viewers had noticed him much prior to the judges' houses phase, because he wasn't shown much on-screen. Even once the band was assembled and thrust into the live shows, Louis was one of its less prominently featured members. In the aftermath of the season, as One Direction took the first steps in its career, his very inclusion in the band was called into question by an embittered past winner of the show. Many people would have been disheartened to have such lesser stature. Not Louis—he kept his head up, continued to display his winning smile, and before long, he was a firm favorite with the fans, sometimes receiving the loudest cheers and screams during concerts and public appearances.

It took some poise and assurance to manage that. As the oldest child in his family, Louis has rarely lacked for either. He has four younger sisters, Phoebe, Daisy, Félicité, and Charlotte. As the first-born, he is expected to have certain inherent characteristics, among which are a strong sense of duty and responsibility, and an ability to lead. This is largely because the oldest child in a family, particularly a large clan like the Tomlinsons, usually has an almost semi-parental role in the home. Louis has stated that people have sometimes been impressed by how well he deals with children. "First borns" can also, on a less positive note, be prone to self-criticism, and feelings of envy and guilt. Behind his carefree image, Louis has moments of unhappiness and uncertainty.

In truth, though, the fact that he is the only boy in the family had as much of an effect on his life as his place in the birth order. It made him very close to his mother, Johanna, from the early days. That fond relationship endures to this day, even when he is thousands of miles away from her. The Tweets between mother and son on Twitter testify to their closeness. So do their pronouncements. "We've got a close relationship," says Johanna. "He's got four sisters and he is my only boy. He is a lovely family lad." With such a large age gap between Louis and his youngest sisters—the twins, Daisy and Phoebe— he was often asked to help with some of the chores around the house, which he did happily. Childhood photos of Louis often show him caring for his sisters. In one famous image, his sister Charlotte is sitting on his lap as he reads her a book. He loves all his sisters, but that does not stop him from wishing he could have had a brother as well. However, not having a brother has given him the opportunity to form a close bond with his dad, as the only males in the crowded Tomlinson household.

All of the band's fans are only too aware that Louis is the chattiest member of One Direction. His love of speaking, speaking, and then speaking some more long preceded the band. Even when he was still in a stroller, Louis would talk for most of the day. Strangers on the street would find themselves greeted loudly by the cute-faced kid in the stroller. If they did not respond with sufficient friendliness, they became victims of a less warmhearted follow-up comment from the loquacious Louis. He was full of so much energy and character—there seemed to be something special about Johanna's "lovely family lad" from the start.

Louis was prone to dreaming as a child. Before he settled on singing as a career, he dreamed of being, among other things, a Power Ranger, a soccer player, a farmer, a drama teacher, and an actor. Louis admits that as a child he became "obsessed" with Power Rangers and for several Christmases running, he had asked for a Power Rangers toy or some other sort of merchandise. When the family moved to Poole, a town near Bournemouth, England, he was thrilled to learn that there were Power Ranger rides on the seafront. His future bandmate Zayn Malik was, unbeknownst to Louis at this time, also a Power Rangers fanatic. A more intriguing coincidence is the fact that the man who would later make the boys' dreams come true, had played a significant part in the Power Rangers story. Simon Cowell, noting the huge success that the television series was achieving, signed a deal to release Power Rangers songs. One of these releases reached number three on the charts. In years to come, Cowell would put Louis at the top of the charts, too.

First, though, Louis had various stages to go through as he developed his love of entertainment. His early love was acting rather than singing. He was soon taking small parts as an extra on television shows. This run in acting began when he needled his way onto the cast of a show in which his twin sisters were appearing. On the set, he met the celebrity James Corden and they remain friends to this day. He took acting classes and was even ambitious enough to make an arrangement with a theatrical agent. Small parts followed, including one in the long-running BBC show *Waterloo Road* and another in a drama called *If I Had You*. Louis also acted in school plays and one of the highlights of his pre-*X Factor* life was when he secured the lead role of Danny in a production of *Grease*. There were 200 people in the audience, and it is reported that he was a reasonably compelling leading man.

Aside from acting, Louis always made an impact at school. He was later remembered vividly—if sometimes with contradictions—by several of the staff who taught him. Louis's school principal, Yvonne Buckley, recognized his familial role when she said, "Louis was a hardworking and determined pupil who is extremely supportive of his sisters." Buckley's memory of Louis as hardworking is challenged by his former teacher, Jenni Lambert. "I'm absolutely delighted for him," she told the *Daily Star*. "He was a bit of a rogue at school at times, but he absolutely loved performing, and the thing he lived for most was performing with the band at assemblies. Performing was what he always wanted. He is a very charming chap, but he wasn't a great fan of doing academic work." That said, she concludes that "He has a very likeable quality." He has provided her with a shining example to use to motivate her students. If they work hard, she tells them, they too could go on to become successful like Louis.

Despite his early acting success—a discipline to which Louis aspires to return one day in the future—it was music that made him the example that Lambert can now use. When he was fourteen he joined a band called The Rogue. He is proud to have been in the band and is very proud of their name (it is certainly more impressive than Harry's White Eskimo). The story of how he joined the band is an unconventional one. The other band members became friendly with Louis during a school trip to

Norfolk, England, and they asked him if he would like to be their lead singer. That they asked him this without even knowing whether he could sing or not says a lot about Louis's inherent star quality. If you wanted to know how to identify a person who has that amazing quality known as "the X factor," then just check out Louis. His charismatic personality—plus, his cute face—was enough to convince an already-formed band that he was the man to lead them.

Fortunately, once he did sing for them, they were happy with what they heard. The Rogue was now complete. Their sound was more "rocky" than that of One Direction. The Rogue performed songs by the American punk-pop stadium band Green Day, who are best known for their anthems "American Idiot," "Wake Me Up When September Ends," and "Good Riddance (Time of Your Life)." The Rogue also tried out songs by another American rock band, The Killers. When Louis sang these bands' songs, he partly imagined himself as their respective lead singers—Billie Joe Armstrong and Brandon Flowers—but, he also made sure to bring himself into the performance.

In time, he would be a real star, with all the benefits that come with that—including girls. When asked about his first kiss, Louis explained to the website Sugarscape.com, "I don't really remember that much about it. It was one of those kind of like ... kind of weird moments. It was all right." His first celebrity crush was on the *Harry Potter* actress Emma Watson. He remembers falling for her when he and his friends went to watch the first *Harry Potter* movie. "Literally all the lads fancied [her]," he said.

As he entered his teenage years, Louis started dating a girl who he "really liked." However, a few weeks later, she ended their relationship because, she told him, he "wasn't good-looking enough." Recounting the story after becoming a heartthrob through One Direction, Louis's pain was still palpable. "It still hurts me inside," he said. His fans nowadays are baffled that any girl could dump their hero.

Even taking into account that Louis is the oldest member of One Direction, his childhood was still a busier and more eventful experience than his bandmates'. He was an energetic boy, wanting to try as many of the things that life offered as possible.

His resume is packed with the many jobs he had. As a teenager, Louis worked as a football coach, selling snacks at a football stadium, as a waiter, at a branch of the well-known chain Toys 'R' Us, and at a movie theater.

Soon, though, it became time for him to apply to audition for *The X Factor*. He applied in 2009, but did not make it past the first round. He spent the next year determined to return and succeed. When he reapplied for the 2010 season, he had just finished his final exams. His life would never be the same again.

3 ZAYN MALIK

With his incredibly handsome features, including his magnificent mane of dark hair, Zayn could have taken a totally different career path. He could easily have become a model. It would have been even easier for him to become arrogant and smug—plenty of good-looking young celebrities are. They quickly realize that their fine features are enough to open doors for them and decide that they have no need to exude any genuine charm. As for Zayn, despite his undeniable slice of vanity, he has avoided these pitfalls and has instead remained the kind, down-to-earth, and slightly eccentric guy that he has always been.

Zayn Malik—his name is also sometimes spelled "Zain"—was born on January 12, 1993. His mom is named Tricia, and his dad's name is Yaser. He comes from a large and friendly family, and has three sisters, five aunts, two uncles, and over twenty cousins. Having so many female relatives (just like his bandmate Louis) has made Zayn particularly empathetic toward women. Not only that, but Zayn is the second oldest sibling in his immediate family, and "middle born" children are believed to have particularly strong sensitivity to the needs of others. His middle-born status also means that Zayn is more inclined to fight on behalf of the weak or the underdog. All of these exciting facts—along with his good looks and success—make him great boyfriend material.

But what kind of childhood did he have? His earliest memory is of a trip to the fair with his mother and grandmother. For the three-year-old Zayn, this was quite an experience. All the lights, noise, and general sense of excitement left a big impression on the toddler. Although Zayn loved being the center of attention at home, on this outing, his attention and his senses were captivated by what was going on around him. As a celebrity, his life is colorful, hectic, and exhilarating most of the time now—a lot like a busy carnival.

He attended Lower Fields elementary school in Bradford, England. The school's motto is "Sharing the Vision, Achieving Success." While he was there, he began to develop the passion that would eventually lead him to global celebrity. "I've always loved singing," he said. During his early school years, Zayn gave one of his first public performances when he sang as part of a choir for the Lord Mayor. He also took part in theatrical pursuits. The principal of Lower Fields, John Edwards, said of his now famous former pupil, "I remember he was a nice young man, hard-working, and I remember in particular his leading role in the Year Six leavers' play."

There were many happy times for Zayn at school. However, as the child of a mixed marriage, he also found his early experiences at school to be challenging. "I almost felt like I didn't fit in at my first two schools because I was the only mixed heritage kid in my class," he wrote in the book *Dare to Dream: Life as One Direction*. This made life uncomfortable, and he eventually moved to a new school where he stood out less and settled in happily. It was here that he also began to notice girls. The first time he kissed a girl, Zayn had to improvise to make the smooch work. "I remember the girl being taller than me and we were outside somewhere so I had to stand on top of a brick to get level with her. That's a major thing I remember about my first kiss." As time went on, Zayn became more and more aware of female charms, including famous women. "My first celebrity crush was definitely Megan Fox," he confessed.

It is no coincidence that it was also about this time that Zayn began to take extra special care in his appearance. Now that he was trying to impress girls, he wanted to look his best. His attention to detail exceeded that of most boys his age. "Vain Zayn" would even happily sacrifice thirty minutes of sleep in the morning to have enough time to perfect his look and style his hair to his highly exacting standards. Perhaps living with so many girls had influenced him to take such a high interest in his appearance. It was actually Zayn's dad who cut his hair as a child, and it was his dad who also helped him get the look right in the morning. All of the attention that was given to Zayn's appearance paid off—he looked amazing.

Zayn experimented with different looks to try and gain attention from girls and to discover his own identity. At one stage, he shaved off his hair and shaved lines into his eyebrows. As a fan of hip hop and R&B, he was trying to look the part. His overall aim was to look "cool" and "tough." In hindsight, he wonders if he ever managed either. He did, however, attract attention from girls, and at the young age of fifteen, he snagged his first girlfriend. Before Zayn became famous, he only had three girlfriends. By then he had developed some basic tastes—he likes girls with loads of character and fun personalities. To Zayn, these characteristics are more important than how a girl looks. Some details of his romantic life, though, will probably always remain secret. When asked for details on past relationships, "A gentleman would never say," Zayn commented.

Zayn's love of singing and performing grew each year. He loved how it felt to perform—it made him come alive and placed him at the center of everyone's attention. It also gave him an outlet for his high level of energy. Zayn was such an energetic child that his mom took him to the doctor to see if there was anything that could be done to calm him down.

At home, he performed in front of his family. He sang songs by many artists, including Daniel

Bedingfield. He didn't know it at the time, but one of Bedingfield's most well-known fans is Simon Cowell—the man who would eventually change Zayn's life.

In addition to singing, Zayn had a flair for acting. In middle school, he landed a part in a production of *Grease*. Due to his small build, a new part had to be created for Zayn because he wasn't big enough to play the lead (as Louis had done at his school). Zayn continued to act in other productions, including the light-hearted gangster story *Bugsy Malone*— in which he played the lead—and the fantasy adventure *Arabian Nights*. He felt that playing the part of someone else, and taking on a new identity, was both liberating and exhilarating. He got such a high from performing that sometimes it took him a while to "come down" afterward and relax enough to sleep. He was experiencing something that hits lots of artists—the "performance high." At least he had new friends to share this experience with. He befriended several of his fellow performers and remains friends with many of them to this day. Despite his busy schedule, Zayn has done his best to stay grounded and he considers consistent contact with his childhood friends to be a very easy and positive way of doing this.

Zayn does not conform to all the characteristics associated with "middle-born" children. For instance, many experts believe that such children tend to excel more in non-academic ways, rather than at school. Zayn has excelled at both. By the age of eight, he was already reading at an adult level. He is also a talented artist—something he believes he inherited from his dad. He is definitely not just a pretty face.

As a Capricorn, Zayn is expected to be ambitious and humorous, yet also shy and reserved. He has certainly shown signs of all these traits. Fans have marvelled at his witty retorts in some situations, yet they have also noticed how he can be quiet and reserved at times. He remembers times during his childhood when he wanted to be in the limelight and capture everyone's attention, yet he also recalls times when he preferred to hide away, alone in a quiet room. These contrasts make Zayn intriguing, and it is these complexities that help give him that intangible but important quality necessary for all successful entertainers: "the X factor."

So, he was obviously a promising candidate for the

talent show of the same name. Having distinguished himself as a "star" at Tong High, he put his courses on hold temporarily to audition for *The X Factor*. The assistant principal, Steve Gates, told the local newspaper, the *Telegraph and Argus,* that Zayn was "a model student who excelled in all the performing arts subjects." He added, "He was always a star performer in all the school productions." It was a music teacher at Tong High who first suggested that Zayn enter the famous talent show. It took him some time to get up the courage to actually go through with the audition. In 2008—the same year that Liam Payne first auditioned, reaching the judges' houses phase—Zayn did obtain an application form but didn't fill it out. The following year, he did the same. The desire to enter the show was strong, but it was overcome by his nerves. He kept asking himself if he really had what it takes. He knew he looked great, but he wondered if his voice would be strong enough and if he had the confidence to get through the contest.

Finally, in 2010, he actually went for it. He filled out the form, sent it, and auditioned. Even then, though, he needed a final piece of encouragement.

On the day of the audition, he changed his mind again. Behind his doubt was a fear that he would be rejected. He wanted to stay in bed. Eventually it was his mom who ordered him to get up and go to the audition. "I was really nervous, but she told me just to get on with it and not miss my chance," remembered Zayn.

What happened next proved that famous saying to be true: mother knows best.

4 NIALL HORAN

When One Direction stormed the charts in America, one of the first people to congratulate the boys on Twitter was the prince of pop himself, Justin Bieber. After congratulating the whole band, the young Canadian heartthrob sent a follow-up Tweet to Niall Horan's account, which read, "Good guys always win, bro." This was a particularly apt message—not only is Niall a long-term admirer of Bieber, but the young Irishman is also one of life's good guys. Loyal, friendly, and witty, Niall has always been a bundle of joy to those who have met him. Bieber is far from alone in his appreciation. Niall does not lack fans who admire his ongoing victories.

So, what was this Irish boy's childhood like? When asked to describe the Horan family, Niall's father probably put it best, "We were just ordinary people." Niall Timothy Horan was born on September 13, 1993. He grew up in the town of Mullingar, in Westmeath, Ireland. The town he was raised in is small and quiet—as Niall himself puts it, there's not much for young people to do there. After all, its main tourist attractions are its lakes, and lakes—even stunningly beautiful ones—are only of limited interest to most teenagers. That said, Niall has remained loyal to the neighborhood since he became internationally famous. He still believes that the best way to spend a night is to go out in town with his best friends. There might not be that much to do, but there is no place like home and no friends like the ones he made as a kid.

The town is very proud of Niall—there have even been requests for a statue of him to be erected there. On a larger scale, he is proud to be an Irishman and to fly the flag for Ireland on the world stage. The only part of that experience that bothers him is when people make ignorant remarks about Ireland, and the Irish in general. For instance, he has complained that people constantly ask him if he likes potatoes—in reference to the Irish potato famine. Although Niall now travels the world with the band, he still feels there is no place like his home nation. As his childhood friend Sean Cullen observed, even in the midst of so much fame, success, and attention, if there is one thing Niall enjoys it is a chance to touch base with his buddies back where he grew up. "He loves coming home," said Cullen.

For the first four years of his life, Niall's family lived in the center of the town. They then moved to an estate farther out of town, but soon after the move, Niall's parents split up. It was a very upsetting time for him and all of the Horan family. However, Niall was young when this happened, so his understanding of the emotional and practical complexities of it was minimal. At first he stayed with his mother, but then moved in with his dad, whose home was located more conveniently near Niall's school. His early memories include playing on the street with his older brother and other kids in the neighborhood. These were not always harmonious times for the siblings, because Niall was always the quintessential younger brother. He was not only younger, he was also short for his age, which only added to his vulnerability.

Not that this stopped the bold Niall from once striking his brother Greg with a ping pong paddle, drawing blood in the process. Some of the toys that Niall enjoyed playing with as a child included a toy tractor, which he drove up and down the street, and an army outfit with a helmet and a huge toy gun. Then, one Christmas, he got a toy car race track. "I must have been about four or five years old and I got a Scalextric thing and that was probably one of the best presents I ever got," he told Capital Radio.

Niall and his brother had pet goldfish that they named after the cartoon characters Tom and Jerry. Unfortunately, Greg overfed them and they died— an upsetting experience for all concerned. There was often tension between the two brothers as they grew up. Niall has said that for many years they "hated each other" but they are now loving siblings.

Niall has more early memories of his life that include playing in his toy tractor, traveling to New York for a family vacation, and crying on the first day of school. He quickly found his confidence at school and became very outgoing and talkative. Full of fun and chatter, he says he "talked a lot during lessons" but never so much that he got into any serious trouble, aside from one occasion when he skipped school for a day, and landed himself in a great deal of trouble.

His favorite subjects were Geography and French; he was less interested in English and Math. Homework was one part of school life that he never quite learned to enjoy. One of his closest friends was a boy named Nicky—they first became friends when Nicky broke wind during a boring geography class. The incident really broke the monotony of the lesson. Nicky could not have known at the time that because of this moment, he would form a lasting friendship with a future internationally famous pop star.

Niall's love of music, the tool that would take him to such celebrity, continued to grow. He learned to play the recorder soon after he started school, and his musical talents continued to develop from there. The first person to note that he had a good singing voice was his music teacher in elementary school, Mrs. Caulfield. Having heard Niall's beautiful voice while he sang Christmas carols, she recommended him for the local town's choir. He was eight years old. His love of—and talent for—singing was also noticed by his family. Once, during a road trip with his aunt, he was sitting in the back of the car singing a song by Garth Brooks. His singing was so good that his aunt told him she thought the radio was on. From that moment, she truly believed that her nephew was going to become a pop star.

As Niall has reflected, a similar car-based experience happened to the world-famous singer Michael Bublé when he was a child. Niall was thrilled by the coincidence. Little did he know that he would one day meet his hero. Aside from being inspired by Bublé, Niall also studied the music and life of Frank Sinatra. Without Sinatra's example, he has said, he would not have become a singer himself. It is touching to know that Niall, a young man who is now inspiring so many people, was inspired by someone in the past. He has long dreamed of a duet with his hero Justin Bieber—and that prospect doesn't seem so unlikely, given where Niall is now.

Two years after he joined the town choir, Niall took his love of singing and performing to a new level. "I've always sung and when I was about ten, I played Oliver in the school play and I just always remember being really happy on stage," he said. In addition to singing and acting, he also learned to play the guitar. Niall's strumming has become a key part of his place within One Direction. He was twelve when he learned to play the instrument. "He learned how to play from the Internet," remembered his father, Robert. When Niall's voice and guitar technique improved, he entered some talent shows. He sang songs such as, "I'm Yours" by Jason Mraz, "Last Request" by Paolo Nutini, and "The Man Who Can't Be Moved" by The Script. Sometimes he entered the contests with his friend Kieron, who would accompany Niall's singing with some guitar playing.

They were an impressive duo. The first talent show they performed in was a local event. Niall, then thirteen, was noticed by the local media, and he got his first taste of publicity when they featured him in articles and photographs. It felt strange, but exciting, to see his name and face in print. He felt genuine pride when he saw the reaction from his family and friends.

The next show he entered he won. He sang Chris Brown's song "With You." His victory gave him sufficient confidence to believe that he could have a future as a professional singer. Further local media coverage followed his participation in a regional *Stars In Their Eyes* show. He had really enjoyed the experience and his confidence was growing. Could his aunt be right? Was he destined to become a pop idol?

Soon, he got to perform actual live shows as an opening act. He opened for 2009 *X Factor* finalist Lloyd Daniels. Niall had been impressed by Daniels' experience on the show and he told him that he was planning to enter himself. Daniels would later claim that he had encouraged Niall to do so, but Niall remembered the exchange differently. As he remembered it, the baby-faced Daniels actually seemed less than impressed when he stated his plan.

Aside from performing, Niall loved listening to music. One of his favorite bands was Westlife. He also became a fan of Justin Bieber and really loves the Jonas Brothers. "They are legends," he says. Little did he know that he would one day meet both of them and then go on to emulate their enormous success.

Niall has had a less eventful love life than some other members of One Direction, but he has still had his encounters with the opposite sex. He had his first kiss with a foreign exchange student who was visiting from France. She was boarding with the family of one of Niall's friends. He also developed a crush on several female celebrities including Jennifer Lopez. He had a girlfriend at one point, but he says that it was not a long-term or serious thing. "I've not actually been on too many dates," he has told *OK!* magazine. "I just like sitting at home, chilling, and watching a movie," he added.

Other memorable moments from Niall's childhood include soccer games on the school fields and a host of memorable hairstyles that now make him cringe. Niall's parents have summed him up succinctly. "He's a lighthearted lad. One thing I do know is that he is completely committed and focused on his singing," said his mother, Maura. "He'd sing for his breakfast, dinner, and tea." Lighthearted is exactly what Niall usually is—there are very few things that can ruffle his easy-going nature. One thing that can, though, is pigeons. His hatred for them began after a hair-raising experience while he was answering the call of nature. "I can't stand them after one once flew in through my bathroom window and went for me. That was enough. I think pigeons target me," he told the *Sun*. Well, why should they be any different from One Direction's millions of fans?

As for his father, Robert, he says that Niall had shown glimpses of other entertainment skills early in life. "Niall was always interested in showbiz," he told the *Irish Independent*. "Apart from singing, he always spent his childhood mimicking others. He's brilliant; he'd have been a stand-up comedian if he hadn't gone down this route. He can pick up any dialect." Niall is frequently the most humorous and entertaining member of One Direction. When the band is working hard on the road, it is often Niall's sense of humor that keeps them going.

However, Niall can be very serious when he needs to be. Don't let his smiling face fool you—he has strong ambition in his soul. Even when he applied to audition for *The X Factor*, Niall, inspired by the success of teenage winner Joe McElderry, seemed to have a sense that he was going to go places. So much so that even though he was dating a girl who he found "amazing," he decided to break up with her shortly before he auditioned for *The X Factor*, believing that his life was about to change dramatically. "I needed to concentrate on my career," he said.

His mom, Maura, has spoken more about this girl and her relationship with Niall. "He had a girlfriend at home, from his school days, before he auditioned for *The X Factor*," she told the *Herald*. "But then he was doing that and she was doing exams, so life is very different for him now. I don't know if he sees much of her when he's home; she was lovely, but they were only sixteen at the time—there's never anything too steady about a relationship at that age." The fact that he ended the relationship shows that Niall clearly was not just auditioning for the hell of it—he meant business. That said, he still had the intelligence to develop some other plans to fall back on in case he did not succeed in the talent show. Having recently finished his exams, he had plans to go to college to study Civil Engineering. However, he is unlikely to follow up on that plan anytime soon. The nice guy of pop has bigger fish to fry nowadays.

5 LIAM PAYNE

If there is a single quality that has shaped the course of Liam Payne's life, it is determination. Not just any type of determination—but a strong, steady resolve. Liam can have fun and melt hearts when the time is right, but he will not let anything get in his way when he seeks to fulfill his goals. Which is just as well, because, like many stars, he has had to overcome several setbacks in his journey to the top. The most significant and challenging of them all is that he was, as he has himself put it, born "effectively dead." Doctors had to work fast to bring him around—a far from ideal start. He arrived into the world on August 29, 1993, a full three weeks premature, and then suffered from a series of health issues during the first four years of his life. The fundamental problem he faced was that he was born with just one functioning kidney. This occurs in about one out of 750 people and creates a number of complications for the sufferer.

When he was born, the doctors didn't get a reaction from him and they feared that he wasn't going to make it. Luckily, he survived this dramatic entrance to the world, but he was still destined for several years of regular hospital visits. At first, the doctors did not know why he kept getting sick. He went in and out of the hospital for tests and examinations as doctors tried to get to the bottom of the problem. Finally, after several years of testing, the doctors discovered Liam's kidney issue. Like most people, Liam has two kidneys, but only one of them worked properly, and in the years that his misfunctioning kidney went undetected, it had become so scarred that there was no hope of saving it and turning it into a healthy, working organ.

Instead, Liam was sentenced to a course of treatment that would be enough to take anyone to the brink of despair. At one stage, he had to have thirty-two injections in his arm each morning and evening. He must have felt like a pincushion as he endured this painful and time-consuming treatment.

As anyone who has undergone complicated medical treatment as a child remembers, the desire for the treatment to be finished and in the past is strong. More than anything, the child just wants to be normal like other children. But despite this, Liam managed to stay happy most of the time, and his mom remembers him dancing around the living room to the theme song from the children's television series *Noddy*.

Eventually, the treatment was scaled back and Liam's life became more normal. He was told that due to his kidney problem, it was more important than ever that he keep himself as healthy as possible. For instance, he couldn't drink too much liquid; even water had to be carefully rationed. He took all the advice the doctors gave him very seriously, and the legacy of that advice has been a considerable factor in everything that has happened in his life ever since. It has kept Liam more focused than most on leading a healthy, successful, and long life.

His first school was Collingwood Infants School, in Wolverhampton, England. Few who were there at the same time will forget Liam, because within days of arriving, he got himself into lots of trouble. He was in and out of the principal's office after a number of pranks, including water fights. He also climbed onto the roof to retrieve soccer balls that had been accidentally kicked up there by over-zealous players. Even though he was playful and impish, Liam did concentrate in class. One of his favorite subjects was Science.

While he was in elementary school, he began to develop a love of music and singing—a love that would eventually change his life forever. When he was just five years old, Liam gave his first public performance. "I've always loved singing, it's something I've always done, ever since I first got up on karaoke when I was at holiday camp and mumbled the words to Robbie Williams 'Let Me Entertain You.'" he explained later. Although his Robbie rendition had not been pitch-perfect, Liam definitely enjoyed it—and the reaction he got—and it made him want to continue developing his voice. His mother was not bothered by the imperfections—she was so proud that she filmed the performance. He has also spoken of another early karaoke performance, in which he sang R Kelly's "I Believe I Can Fly."

At home, Liam had plenty of love. His father,

Geoff, and mother, Karen, also had two daughters, Nicola and Ruth, both of whom are older than Liam. They, too, enjoy singing. Nicola is the oldest of the siblings. To Liam, she was an authority figure. As the youngest sibling, Liam is a "last born" child. Experts who have studied birth order have identified a number of characteristics that are common in last borns, among which are extra reserves of charm and a strong desire to be the center of attention. Such children are also often strongly creative, but less ambitious and organized than others. They are said to be rebellious and willing to take risks.

How much of this can we see in Liam? Clearly, his charm is undeniable. He supplements his good looks with an allure and charisma that comes from deeper in his soul. As for a desire to be center of attention, he has this only partially. Clearly, he is comfortable under the spotlight of the stage and television cameras. However, in more everyday social situations, he can be the relatively shy and introverted. Many have identified Liam as "the quiet one" of the band. Is he rebellious, creative, and risk-taking? As we shall see, yes, he is. However, one last-born characteristic that could not apply less to Liam is a lack of ambition.

More than any member of One Direction, Liam has a clearly set objective that he has been focused on for several years.

He is so ambitious that he has had more than one goal in his life and he has considered a number of different career paths before he turned to music. He tried—and failed—to get onto the school soccer teams so, instead, he decided to try running. His first attempt was a cross-country race and to his delight, Liam both enjoyed the feeling of running and also came in first place.

This sweet feeling was temporarily soured when Liam was accused, quite unfairly, of cheating. He had been up against one of the region's best athletes, someone who spectators were amazed that Liam, a mere newcomer, had managed to beat. The following week, Liam challenged the same runner to a repeat race. Again, Liam beat him. Now there could be no doubt about his ability. He quickly became a fanatical runner. He loved it all—the feeling of freedom in the open air, the fact that it kept him fit, the sense of achievement, and the natural high he felt at the end of a race. He joined the Wolverhampton and Bilston Athletics Club. He was truly committed to running and would frequently wake up as early as 6 A.M. to run about six miles before school, as well as another couple of miles in the early evening.

All the training paid off. By the time he was twelve, Liam had become such an accomplished and successful runner, that he was put in his school's under-eighteen team. There he was, not yet a teenager, competing successfully with men who were eighteen years old. At his club, Liam continued to compete too, and for three years, he finished in the top three for his age group in 1,500-meter runs. As Liam himself said, these achievements are "amazing." He came agonizingly close to getting a place on the England running team. It is quite possible that, if he got that spot, we would know him not as a member of One Direction, but as a member of Team GB at the London 2012 Olympics.

Running was just one sport that Liam was involved in. Thanks to regular family vacations in America, he had become a basketball fan. He joined a local team, but soon found himself targeted by some older boys who were jealous of Liam's snazzy American gear. However, the bullying went beyond just nasty words. Liam became so scared and upset that he shared his concerns with his family. One of his sisters was dating a former boxer at the time, and Liam's parents suggested that he also learn to box, so the bullies would think twice about picking on him in the future.

People who have kidney problems are often advised to avoid contact sports, but Liam was cleared to try out boxing. Once he got to the boxing club, he was thrown in at the deep end. One of his first fights, when he was twelve, was against a thirty-eight-year-old boxing trainer. No wonder Liam's early visits to the boxing club were such scary experiences. He would often arrive home shaken-up and bruised—he even suffered a broken nose and a perforated eardrum. But he still kept going—most weeks he was there three times.

However, fighting skills aside, he was also gaining the very thing he had gone there for: confidence. The bullies continued to be nasty to him for a while, including chasing him down the street one day. They were cowards in every sense. They were older than Liam and acted in a pack. When Liam's patience snapped, he had a fight with one of them and, thanks to his boxing training, he won. He got in lots of trouble at school in the aftermath, with expulsion being one of the options he was threatened with. He showed the world that he was not going to tolerate being pushed around, though.

Other sports that Liam enjoyed included soccer, as both a player and a fan—despite his disappointment at not making it onto the school team. He has always been a true, passionate devotee of the beautiful game. Liam also appreciated Physical Education classes. In fact, he enjoyed them so much that it was suggested to him that he should consider becoming a gym teacher. It was an option that was of some interest to him.

Liam always seemed to be concentrating on his future. While he cherished the experience of being a kid, he always had an eye on what was to come. Other career paths he considered included an apprenticeship at the aircraft factory where his father worked. Liam imagined it would be a lot like playing giant Lego games all day, though his Dad was quick to tell him that it was very tough work. He even thought about becoming a businessman. Liam became so inspired by entrepreneurs he'd seen on television, that he started a small venture of his own. He bought large bags of candy and then sold them at school for a profit. Young Liam frequently made a profit of around $80 a week.

In fact, Liam's childhood business experiences gave him a fixed view on how young people should conduct their lives. "Young people should stay in school and get qualifications," he told *The Sunday Times*. "You can't just sit around doing nothing. They should get out there and make things happen," says Liam. He is not the only One Direction member to admire and favor young enterprise. Harry, too, has spoken out in similar terms. He said that young people "should become entrepreneurs, make a job for themselves, start a company."

Liam went through several hairstyles as a kid. These included a buzz cut, a tramlines style, and what he called "a big mushroom." Eventually, he settled on the popular fringe. He began to notice girls as he grew up, and recalls that his first kiss was with a girl named Vicky. "She was a lovely girl," he recalled. He also recalled a girl named Charnelle who used to send him love letters. She was two years older than him and Liam felt quite grown-up dating an older girl. None of these girls knew they were encountering a future star who would soon become a heartthrob to girls across the planet.

He also developed a huge crush on a girl named Emily and asked her out over twenty times before she said yes. He only secured a positive response after singing to her. The song he chose was Mario's "Let Me Love You." "She dumped me the next day because I had pressured her into it by singing to her," he said. It may surprise some of his fans to learn that before he was famous, Liam, now adored by millions of girls worldwide, was actually often unlucky in love. Sometimes he was told by friends that a particular girl was interested in him. It was only after he confidently asked the girl out and was turned down that he discovered his friends had just been pranking him. "Mortifying" was how he put it.

Meanwhile, music was still a big part of Liam's life. That elementary school performance of "Let Me Entertain You" had proved to be just the start of his love affair with music. He certainly enjoyed listening to it—his favorite artists included Robbie Williams and Oasis, the lyrics of the latter matching Liam's outlook on life. "You've gotta make it happen," sing Oasis in one of their songs. Liam agreed. He also enjoyed singing, so he joined the school choir when he was in ninth grade. With the choir, Liam got plenty of experience singing in front of an audience. They even set a world record when they, and several other schools, joined to sing the same song—"Lean On Me" by Bill Withers—in unison.

Liam didn't only sing in the choir. During family outings, he would sing in the car, and then at home, he would put on a pair of sunglasses and sing along to his dad's Oasis CDs. Showing his natural sense of performance, Liam would copy the posture of the band's lead singer, Liam Gallagher—hands tucked behind his back, neck tipped so his face pointed upward. In those moments, he did his best to imagine what it would be like to actually perform a concert in front of thousands of fans.

Liam's other big inspiration is American singer Usher, the man who helped launch the career of Justin Bieber, whom Liam would be compared with when his own career began.

Always the type of person to take his interests to the next level, when he was twelve, Liam joined a local performing arts group called Pink Productions. His teacher there, Jodie Richards, remembered her encounters with the future heartthrob. "Liam joined us as a timid boy who wanted to sing after watching his sisters perform with us," she told the *Express & Star* newspaper. She never doubted his talent but found that he needed an injection of confidence to match it. "Who'd have thought the Liam we see today would have nearly had to be forced onto the stage? It was clear very early that Liam was a natural talent." She added that he gained more and more confidence with each show and tackled some "big singing numbers." Assessing his overall character, she described him as a lovely boy and explained that she is proud to be able to say she knows him.

Liam continued to take any chance he could to sing in public. He sang karaoke in America, England, Spain, and Portugal. He had almost performed a world tour of sorts long before One Direction had been formed. Through these performances and others, Liam gradually became more accomplished. His voice improved and so did his overall stage presence. (Of all the future members of One Direction, Liam would make best use of the stage at his first 2010 *X Factor* audition.) That confidence onstage was honed during these performances in the years leading up to it.

Liam listened to the feedback he was given and perfected his persona. When he first entered *X Factor* in 2008, his friends teased him, but it was only friendly banter. At heart, they wished him the best. He got more and more excited as the big date grew closer. He really wanted to do well. "People had told me that I was a good singer so I thought I would give it a go and audition for *X Factor*," he said.

That said, for a boy who would go on to become an international heartthrob, Liam certainly chose an interesting outfit for his first television appearance. He wore a shirt that was too big for him, making the collar appear almost comically oversized, underneath a jacket. His jeans were also too big for him, so he had to tie his belt really tight just to hold them up. Although viewers were unaware that one of the shoes he was wearing had a hole in it, it only added to Liam's discomfort as he waited for many hours to get his chance to sing in front of the judges—Simon Cowell, Cheryl Cole, and Louis Walsh.

However, he did not let his ridiculous clothing combination dent his confidence, and he arrived in the audition room looking very composed. "I'm here to win," he told the judges, throwing down the gauntlet from the start. "A lot of people have told me I'm a good singer and that I've got the X Factor—but I don't really know what the X Factor is and I believe you guys do," he said. It was a strong and confident opening line. Simon Cowell, in particular, admires those whose ambitions are high, but equally dislikes any sense of delusion or desperation. Liam had pitched himself well. Afterward, Liam said he felt "a bit nervous" before he started singing, but then the nerves disappeared. He sang the song "Fly Me to the Moon," snapping to the beat with his fingers, and even at one point winking at Cheryl Cole. She appreciated the moment and beamed back in approval.

All in all, it had been a more than adequate performance. When it was time for the judges' verdicts, it was Cowell's opinion that Liam was most interested in. He was more than a little in awe of the head judge and was dying to receive his widely coveted nod of approval—and he knew that Cowell did not offer praise easily. It was Cowell who spoke first, saying he saw "potential" in Liam, but felt that he lacked "a bit of emotion." Cole said she liked Liam and, in contrast to Cowell, was impressed by the "charisma" he showed. Louis Walsh, too, was charmed by the youngster. "I think he could do really well," he said.

Cowell then spoke again. He told Liam he is "a young guy, good looking—people will like you," but added that there was "twenty percent missing for me at the moment." Here, Liam's self-assurance came to the forefront. Rather than buckling under Cowell's observation, he rose to the occasion. "Well, give me another audition and I'll show you I've got that twenty percent," he said. Cole was visibly impressed by this answer, which Liam had delivered with just the right balance of confidence and politeness. When it came to the vote, all three judges said "yes"—Liam had done it! He left the room and was mobbed by his family.

Moving forward, Liam showed his maturity when he continued to take Cowell's criticism in the constructive spirit in which it had been offered. "[Cowell's feedback] gave me something to work on, which is good," he said. Given that some contestants much older than Liam threw tantrums when they were criticized by the panel, Liam's mature reaction was all the more admirable.

The next stage in Liam's journey was the boot camp phase of the show. Here, Liam got the chance to mingle with fellow hopefuls. His ambitious instinct told him that it was worth talking to as many people as possible. He turned out to be a great networker. "People think it's just a singing competition, but it's so much more than that," he said, explaining how much he had enjoyed the overall experience, particularly the chance to make so many new friends.

Then, he sang onstage in front of the judges and gave it his all. The judges were impressed. "Very convincing, very professional and you're only fourteen," Walsh told him. "Liam, you're a little dark horse," added Cowell, prompting a proud yet bashful smile from Liam. Later, the contestants were gathered as the first dreaded cut was delivered. Although many of the contestants were extremely anxious as they waited to find out if they had survived the cut, Liam said he felt "confident."

Once again, his instinct was on-target—he was through to the next stage of boot camp. He was, he recalled, "slightly more nervous" on this day. He sang Elton John's "Your Song." Putting emotion and drama into the performance, he delivered the song with some theatrical moments, wanting the judges to see the full range of his abilities, and to show Cowell that the "missing twenty percent" had been found. After finishing his song, Liam had to leave the stage and let the judges decide their verdict. When he had left, Cowell told his fellow judges, "I like him."

With Cowell's verdict always so weighty, it seemed to viewers that Liam would be safely through to the next, all-important, judges' houses phase. However, it was not that simple. First, the contestants were called to the stage in groups, where they lined up and listened as the judges told them whether they had made it through to the next stage, or whether they would be going home. As usual, the judges injected as much drama as possible into these moments. One favorite trick is to tell the contestants "It's bad news" only to add, following an agonizing pause, a follow-up statement such as, "You'll have to put up with us a bit longer—you're through!"

When Liam stood alongside his fellow contestants, he listened intently to Cowell's words. "Whatever happens, you can leave with your heads held high," the head judge told them, but added, "It's bad news." Even as they left the stage, Liam momentarily turned back to the judges. Perhaps he was hoping for a last-moment twist. Backstage, he was distraught. He said he thought he had done enough to move forward, and said, "I feel like something's been taken away from me." The judges were then shown talking about Liam. "I'm telling you, I think this kid's got a shot," said Cowell. He then ruled that they would put Liam through after all. "I promise you, this is the right decision," he said. The other judges were happy to go along with it.

A producer approached Liam and told him that the judges wanted him to return to the stage. Naturally, he looked shocked. He had watched past episodes of the show and knew that there were always a few "twists" to increase the drama. While he hoped he was returning to the stage to be told he was back in the competition, he knew he could not afford to count on anything. Cowell broke the silence when Liam appeared on the stage, looking a little sheepish. "I don't often do this, but it was such a close call," Cowell began. Liam then interrupted to make a final plea for himself: "I want to take it all the way, Simon."

"I know you do," Cowell replied. "And the other

thing I want to say to you is: we've changed our minds." Liam was so shocked and overjoyed that he sank straight to his knees. "I'd have really, really been mad if I had gone home and not done this," said Cowell. Liam was the "comeback kid!" He had already called home to tell them he was out, so when he made a second call to tell his family that he was, now, through to judges' houses, they didn't believe him at first. "No, I'm being serious—I got through! I'm being super serious," he said. What a roller-coaster day it had been. A touching moment came when Liam's fellow contestants were seen cheering him on. He had won over more than the judges at boot camp.

After believing his *X Factor* journey was over, Liam was now being told of the arrangements for his trip to Barbados to sing in front of Simon Cowell in the judges' houses stage. He knew there was hard work to come, but he also knew that if he got through this round, he would be through to the live shows. The fact that his category was being mentored by his favorite judge only added to Liam's excitement. His category was very strong, including an Irish boy named Eoghan Quigg and other major contenders, including Austin Drage and Scott Bruton.

Alongside Cowell in Barbados was his long-term sidekick Sinitta. She appeared before Liam and the other boys wearing a golden swimsuit that left little to the imagination. "What are you *wearing*?" asked Cowell. Everyone had a good laugh and then it was time to be serious. Liam was asked if he was nervous and he insisted he felt fine. He was again proving his high level of maturity for a boy his age. He sometimes played basketball during his spare time in Barbados. He reflected that he had something in common with Troy, the character that Zac Efron plays in *High School Musical*. Like Troy, Liam was attempting to balance a love of basketball with a love of singing. "The story of *High School Musical* is basically my story," he said. He sang the ballad "A Million Love Songs" and, for his second song he sang, "Hero" by Enrique Iglesias. Dressed all in white, he looked every inch the part of an angelic pop star. After he finished, Sinitta seemed smitten. "Love him," she said. "He has such a cute face—nice little voice as well."

After the performance, Liam said he was sure he had done all he could. "I'm happy with that—I'll settle for that," he said. There was a long night ahead for Liam and the other contestants. They had to sit and wait while, safely out of their earshot, Cowell and Sinitta narrowed down the six remaining contestants to the three who would go through to the live shows. Liam said he felt numb while waiting for Cowell's verdict. Reflecting on what he had been through, he said that as he had passed each stage, his desire to win was only strengthened. "I kept thinking: I want this more, I want this more," he said.

However, it was decision time, and Cowell told Liam, "You look almost like the perfect pop star. I've made a decision—it's bad news." Again, Liam tried to argue his case. This time, though, it didn't work—he was out. Cowell admitted to *Xtra Factor* presenter Holly Willoughby afterward that he had "teetered on the edge" of putting Liam through. When Liam watched the show later, he drew significant comfort from learning how close he had come, but he still found the rejection very difficult to take. He went home and started to pick up the pieces. Cowell had advised him to continue to work on his singing, and then return in two years. Liam prepared to do just that. He launched a website to promote himself and participated in all the live singing opportunities he could.

He had certainly captured public attention. Girls swooned over his good looks, while both his voice and determination had impressed lots of viewers. The day after the judges' houses phase was broadcast, he was invited onto Lorraine Kelly's morning show to discuss his experiences on *The X Factor*. Reflecting on his experience of visiting Barbados overall, Liam quipped, "Well, it was all right until I sunburnt my feet," adding that he had tried to be careful with the sunscreen but that it had "never occurred" to him that his feet could burn.

Kelly asked him who he thought might win the season. In his answer, he showed breathtaking understanding of the pop market. Singling out boy band JLS as strong candidates for victory, he said, "There's no black group currently—there's a gap in the market for one. They're a bit like Boyz II Men so they've got the international edge." JLS emerged runners-up at the end of the season, but the scale of their success made them the *de facto* winners. It was amazing that Liam, then fifteen, had so accurately and wisely assessed their appeal and potential.

Liam's disappointment at being sent home was still palpable and could not be avoided or ignored. "It was so close—it was hard to take," he told Lorraine Kelly. She commented on his overall confidence during his time in the competition and he said it was because he enjoyed singing—so why be nervous about something he enjoyed? As always, Liam's response was straightforward and common sense. He said he would "love to" reapply for the 2009 season. (As it turned out, this would not be possible, as the lower age limit would be raised back to sixteen for 2009 and he would still be fifteen at the crucial cut-off point.)

Still, he certainly planned to return before long and was hopeful that he could go further next time. He pointed out that the 2008 *Britain's Got Talent* teenage winner, George Sampson, had to go through two seasons of the show before he emerged as the winner. For Liam, this was a huge encouragement. Comparing his first *X Factor* experience to school he predicted that his second try would be like an exam. "All I've got to do now," he said, looking forward to his second stab at *The X Factor*, "is pass the exam."

He would do so—with flying colors.

6 IT'S TIME TO FACE THE MUSIC!

The X Factor has faced many controversies and criticisms since the first episode aired on September 4, 2004. Most recently, it has competed with shows that have attempted to knock it off its lofty perch. However, at the time of this writing, it remains Britain's leading talent show and one that makes an almost obscene amount of revenue for all parties concerned. True to the drama that Cowell likes to create on the show, as a franchise it has had its ups and downs. Nowadays, one of the show's proudest achievements is that it launched the career of One Direction.

The X Factor was conceived, created, and launched by Simon Cowell. He had first come to fame—and infamy—on the reality show *Pop Idol*, which was launched in 2001. Previously unknown outside of the inner circles of the British record industry, Cowell quickly distinguished himself as the show's "Mr. Nasty," speaking with such honesty and wit that he quickly became the star of the show. Some hated him for his bluntness, others loved him for it—but nobody was ignoring him. Through two seasons of *Pop Idol,* he became a national celebrity. His fame was then extended to the United States where his put-downs on *American Idol* shocked and delighted viewers who were more accustomed to relentless positivity and political correctness.

Meanwhile, back in Britain, Cowell was enjoying his fame, but was also plotting how to take things one step further. As a judge on *Pop Idol* he had become famous, but his financial ambitions know no bounds. So he devised *The X Factor*—a show that he would not only judge, but also own and run. It has launched the careers of artists such as Leona Lewis, Alexandra Burke, G4, Olly Murs, and JLS. True, there have also been some flops, including Steve Brookstein and Leon Jackson. Other finalists, like Joe McElderry, have stuttered before finding a degree of fame, their success coming as much in spite of, as because of, their association with the show.

Of the several significant differences between *Pop Idol* and *The X Factor*, the most pertinent to One Direction is that in the latter show, bands are allowed to audition. This gives *The X Factor* a new dimension. That said, bands have not always found the experience to be smooth sailing. With reality television competitions so focused on the dramatic background stories of their competitors, bands have found it difficult to create suitable intensity for themselves. While some bands made a success of the show—most notably the aforementioned G4 and JLS who both finished runners-up in their respective seasons—many found that they were voted out very quickly once the live shows began. It was only in the 2011 season that a band actually won the show— the girl band Little Mix. This was a band that had been assembled during the season, in front of the viewers' eyes. The judges and producers had judged that several girls who had auditioned separately as solo singers would be best if they formed a band. It was this very tactic that had brought together One Direction.

Each member of One Direction auditioned as a solo artist in 2010. As we have seen, for some of them, this was not their first experience with the show. The band member with the most significant history with the show was, of course, Liam Payne. We left him in the previous chapter recovering from the rejection he received in the 2008 season. He was channeling that disappointment into something positive—a renewed ambition to make it as a solo pop star. Thanks to the momentary low-level fame his 2008 *X Factor* experience had offered him, he had something to build on. But he was not done with *The X Factor* yet. In fact, he was determined to give the talent show another crack. Even the concerns of some friends and family members—who feared Liam would be devastated if he was rejected again—was not enough to stop him.

A journalist from a local paper, who met with Liam after his 2010 audition, described the way he had successfully updated his image. The journalist recalls him "looking more like a star, rocking trendy tops, skinny jeans, and a super-styled hairdo." He had worked hard between the two auditions, both academically and musically. He took eleven courses at St. Peter's Collegiate School and then moved on to study music technology at Wolverhampton College's Paget Road campus. He had made quite a few public performances after his participation in the 2008 *X Factor* season, including one in front of 29,000 fans at Molineux Stadium, the home of Wolverhampton Wanderers Football (soccer) Club. Surprisingly, he had even appointed men he described as "managers" to guide his fledgling career.

After gearing up to audition again in 2010, Liam was a natural choice to be interviewed and featured on-screen. Many viewers remembered him from the last time around and *The X Factor* has always enjoyed returning contestants. They add to the "soap opera" feel that Simon Cowell likes to establish on the show. Liam was asked about his rejection in Barbados. "I think Simon made the right decision; it has given me the time to work on what I do," he said. "Doing the live shows when I was fifteen, I think I would have struggled to cope. I had never been on a big stage, but now I have much more experience and I am really thankful to Simon for allowing me that. Everything happens for a reason. I'm now a lot more grown up and have performed in front of big audiences."

That said, he was not denying that the rejection hit hard. "It was gutting," he explained, "I know what it's like to be thrown out." Openly stating his priority for this audition, he admitted there was one man he wanted to impress most. He said it would "mean the world" to be given a yes vote by Cowell. And it was Cowell whom Liam first addressed when he took the stage. "How you doing, Simon, you all right?" he asked casually. "Haven't seen you in a long time!" He then confirmed it had been two years since he last auditioned, at which point he "made it through to Simon's house in Barbados." He was coming across as very relaxed and confident. Inside, though, he was not quite so calm. In fact, he wrote later, he actually felt that being up on the stage in front of the judges was "bizarre" and "surreal." He told the panel that he was going to sing "Cry Me a River." Cole assumed he meant the Justin Timberlake song, but within seconds, the opening chords of the Michael Bublé track rang out.

At the end of the song, he got a standing ovation from both the audience and the judging panel— even, he was particularly delighted to note, Simon

Cowell had raised to his feet, a rare and significant occurrence. Liam was stunned—he almost burst into tears there and then, as his emotions bubbled over. He composed himself enough to listen to what the judges had to say. Cheryl Cole was the first to speak. "Whatever 'it' is, you've got it," she told him, to his delight. "And I thought your voice was really, really powerful." Guest judge Natalie Imbruglia agreed, saying Liam was "impressive, really, really impressive," and adding that other contestants should be "a little bit worried about you." Louis Walsh told Liam he was "really, really glad" he had come back. Three judges in a row had used the words "really, really" to emphasize their approval of Liam. However, the judge whose approval he "really, really" wanted was, of course, Simon Cowell.

Walsh handed the conversation over to Cowell, boyishly taunting him with a reminder that "this is the guy you didn't put through!" Cowell confirmed that Liam "wasn't quite ready when he came to my house two years ago," and explained how he had advised him to come back two years later. "I got it right," said Cowell, never missing a moment to brag. Then it was time for the judges to vote "yes" or "no." Given the standing ovation, and the gushing comments, there was no doubt about the outcome in the viewers' minds. However, for Liam, this was still a moment of enormous satisfaction and vindication. Each of the judges' "yes" votes thrilled him. None more so than Cowell's final verdict: "Based on talent—absolutely incredible," he told Liam. "One massive, fat, almighty yes." It was an emotional moment for Liam—you could almost see the disappointment of his 2008 rejection lift from his shoulders.

Liam then returned backstage where presenter Dermot O'Leary was waiting with the Payne family. "You were absolutely tremendous," Liam's mom told him. O'Leary, who remembered the boy well from 2008, seemed almost as overjoyed and proud as the Paynes. "The boy becomes a man," he told Liam, who replied that he felt "really good" that he "waited two years to get up there and do that." Liam was so thrilled that he said "my face hurts" from smiling. In his wildest dreams, he explained, he had never expected to get such an overwhelmingly positive reaction from the judges. He had exceeded his highest hopes and was through to the next round.

"You know, it was so amazing," he said. "Simon stood up for me and that's just the most amazing thing in the world, ever."

In the wake of the audition, he looked back at its true significance. "It has totally changed my life," he said. Liam added that if he hadn't auditioned, he "would probably be working in a factory now." He had still more excitement to come, like when he sat down with his family to watch his audition on national television. "It was brilliant," he said. "My family are so supportive of me and so proud." When he had left that audition he had vowed to give the next stage (boot camp) of the competition his absolute best. He was ready for the rest of the experience. As we have seen, Liam used the boot camp phase of the competition in 2008 as a networking opportunity. This time, he would not only make four new best friends, but he would end up in a band with them.

Harry auditioned in Manchester, England. Although he had sung onstage in front of audiences with White Eskimo, this was a whole new experience for him—there was a 3,000-strong live audience, television cameras, and, of course, the judges. Even for calm Harry, a potentially nerve-wracking experience awaited him. Good thing he had plenty of support with him in the form of an entourage of family and friends, who each wore a T-shirt bearing the slogan "We think Harry has The X Factor!" As for Harry, he was wearing a white T-shirt with a loose grey cardigan, and a green, patterned scarf.

"People tell me I'm a good singer," Harry told host O'Leary. Pointing to Anne, he said, "It's usually my mom." O'Leary commented "And they always say that!" to which Harry readily agreed. "Singing is what I want to do and if people who can make that happen for me don't think that I should be doing that then that's a major setback in my plans." He admitted he was "nervous" as well as "excited," adding that he felt that only if the judges gave him the thumbs-up would he fully believe that he had talent. Lots of friends had praised his voice, but he needed praise from the judges to fully believe that his friends were not lying to make him feel better.

As he waited to go onstage, Harry said the feeling was "surreal"—the same word Liam had used to sum-up the experience. He was showered with kisses just before he left for the stage, something he found "a bit embarrassing." Even O'Leary commented on the awkwardness of the moment, asking "Anyone else want to kiss him?" Onstage he appeared confident and comfortable, saying a cheery "Hello!" to the judges. But, he admitted later that he was a mess inside. His nerves gave him a huge rush of energy and a natural high. He sang "Isn't She Lovely" by Stevie Wonder. This is a song he loved for years and one that he practiced hard so he could perfect his delivery. Unlike most who audition with backing tracks, Harry chose to sing his *a cappela*—without any background music. He got a good round of applause at the end. Although the reaction was tame in comparison to the near hysteria that had greeted Liam's audition, it was still a very positive response. Harry took a smiling bow in response.

He would have cause for some inner applause when he heard the verdict of guest Nicole Scherzinger. She told him, "I'm really glad that we had the opportunity to hear you *a cappela*, because we could really hear how great your voice is. For sixteen years old, you have a beautiful voice." Harry, no stranger to the charms of women, smiled flirtatiously as he thanked her. Next to speak was Louis Walsh. As the man who guided the careers of boy bands Boyzone and

Westlife, his verdict on a young male singer carried a certain amount of extra weight. Sadly, although it began on a positive, it included a major rider. "I agree with Nicole," said the Irishman. "However, I think you're so young. I don't think you have enough experience or confidence yet." Some members of the audience, which for the most part, had really enjoyed Harry's song, were less than impressed with Walsh's verdict, and let him know as much.

Cowell, always up for a chance to tease his old friend Walsh, picked up on this as he took his turn to speak. "Someone in the audience just said 'rubbish' and I totally agree with them," he said. "Because the show is designed to find someone, whether you're fifteen, sixteen, seventeen—it doesn't matter. I think with a bit of vocal coaching you could actually be very good." Harry's smile following these comments was adorable—the judges had yet to deliver their final verdicts, but he had already received the vindication he was hoping for. That said, he wanted to be put through to the next stage, so he anxiously waited for the judging panel's votes.

Walsh, on the left of the panel, spoke first. "Harry, for all the right reasons I am going to say no," he said. There was shock, upset, and outrage from the audience in response. Cowell encouraged the audience to "boo" Walsh as loud as they could. As they did, Harry himself playfully joined in with his own quick "boo." A world away from the fiery responses of the contestants who receive a negative on the show, it was a moment of playful defiance. In all fairness, he could afford to be laid back about it because the other two judges had already given a good indication that they would put him through. Walsh's "no" vote was quickly overruled by the fact that Cowell and Scherzinger both gave Harry a resounding "yes." "I like you, Harry," Scherzinger told him, much to Harry's delight. The moment he realized he had got through to boot camp was, he said, one of the best moments of his life. He made it through, and as he returned to his family, friends, and supporters backstage, he found them bubbling with excitement. Harry was so thrilled, he was struck by a strange paranoia that somehow the decision would be changed. But, there was no chance of that happening.

Harry wasn't the only future member of the band whose first audition split the panel—the same happened when Niall auditioned in Dublin, Ireland. He was living on pure adrenalin on audition day because he was unable to sleep the night before. He knew it was important to get as much sleep as possible the night before such an important, exciting, and potentially draining day, but sleep just would not come. In the end, he simply gave up trying and got up to get ready. He wore a plaid shirt, blue jeans, and sneakers. He arrived at the Convention Centre Dublin at the crack of dawn. He was so excited and nervous.

Like Harry, Niall was interviewed on camera prior to his audition. He mentioned that he had been compared to Justin Bieber and added "it's not a bad comparison." He said he wanted to sell out arenas, record albums, and work with "some of the best artists in the world." He said that his audition was the starting point of all that. "If I get through today—it's game on!" he said. He was coming across as very confident—almost cocky. But, truth be told, everything that has happened to him since then has solidified that confidence.

As he walked onstage he greeted the crowd with a cheeky "All right, Dublin?" Then he told Louis Walsh, "I'm here today to be the best artist I can be in the world." His fellow countryman then asked,

"So are you an Irish Justin Bieber?" Niall agreed that he was. After that, he joked a little with guest judge Katy Perry. He was so amazed to find himself joking with an internationally famous singer such as Perry.

When it came time for him to begin his audition, he sang the Jason Mraz hit "I'm Yours." Simon Cowell, who had heard so many people audition with this song over recent years, told Niall it was a lazy song to select and asked if he had a second song to perform instead. Niall said he did, and then sang "So Sick" by Ne-Yo. There was some symbolism to this—it was one of the songs that Justin Bieber sang at the Stratford Star talent contest, which, indirectly, made him famous. Niall sang it well, but slightly forgettable. His eyes seemed fixed on the back of the venue during the song, in contrast to his future bandmates who all directed their attention and energy on the judges during their respective auditions.

Had he done enough to impress the judging panel? He could not wait to find out. Perry told Niall, "I think you're adorable! You've got charisma—I just think that maybe you should work on it. You're only sixteen. I started out when I was fifteen and I didn't make it until I was twenty-three." A slightly mixed verdict, and one that made her final vote hard to predict. Cowell, too, was ambiguous. "I think you're unprepared. I think you came with the wrong song, you're not as good as you thought you were, but I still like you," he told Niall, who must have been finding it hard to know how to take such confusing responses.

Could Cheryl Cole offer a more positive critique? The pop star said, "Yeah, you're obviously adorable. You've got a lot of charm for a sixteen-year-old, but the song was too big for you, babe." Everyone seemed to have a "but" attached to any praise they gave Niall.

The final judge to speak was Louis Walsh. As a fellow Irishman, and a man who specializes in managing boy bands, he would be, Niall hoped, more likely to appreciate him. "No, I think you've got something," Walsh said. "I think that people will absolutely like you because you're likeable." In the history of *The X Factor*, that has to rank as one of the more eccentric verdicts. Cowell immediately leapt on it, saying, in a sarcastic tone, "So, people will like him because he's likeable?" The audience burst out laughing and so did Niall. "Ah, shut up," snapped Walsh in reply.

When it came to voting time, it was hard to know what each judge would say. It was Cowell who spoke first. "Well, I'm going to say yes," he explained. Niall punched the air and then kissed his hand and crossed himself. He was quickly deflated when Cole followed with a "no." Poor Niall looked absolutely gutted. Perry should have been next to speak but Walsh jumped in and told Niall, "I'm going to say yes!" Contestants need a majority verdict from the panel, meaning that a "yes" from Perry would be enough to send him through. "So now," explained a typically excitable Walsh, "he needs three yeses!" Perry montioned a stabbing motion into her own neck, signifying how much pressure she now felt. Cowell, who was sitting observing all of this drama, loved it. Moments of tension like this are right up his alley. He chuckled at the mischief that Walsh had whipped up.

Perry was less excited about the situation she had been thrust into. Her heart was telling her to put this sweet boy through—but her head was reminding her that she had a responsibility to judge with integrity. "Can I just say that I agree with Cheryl, you do need more experience, and, by the way, just if you're likeable—likeableness is not going to sell records. It's talent—and you have a seed of it." She then paused for a moment, prompting Walsh—who by this stage seemed nearly as anxious as Niall—to plead, "Go ooonnnn!" Perry took one more moment to consider, then said, "Of course, you're in." Niall was so thrilled he leapt in the air and began to cheer. As his microphone picked up his cheer it came out surprisingly deep, compared to his singing voice. "Don't let us down," Perry warned him as he left the stage. After Niall had left, the panel continued to discuss his audition. "He's got charm," said Cowell. "He's got something."

Niall certainly did them proud. After his career with One Direction had made him a success in the U.K., U.S., and beyond, Perry Tweeted him, "Congratulations, you didn't let me down! xo."

Competitors often describe their experience on *The X Factor* as their "journey." Although this has become a horrible cliché—so much so that Cowell even banned the word from being used during one season—in some cases it is literally true. For Zayn, his "journey" began with . . . a long journey. To get to his audition he had to leave at 2 A.M., and to prepare himself for such an early start, he went to bed at four o'clock the previous afternoon. His uncle drove him down to Manchester, England where, like Harry, Zayn auditioned and sang *a cappela*, rather than to a backing track. He had decided to sing the Mario song, "Let Me Love You." An R&B classic, this is a song that has been a hit in several countries. He felt nervous as he prepared to walk onto the stage. Once he did, his nerves worsened. As if the size of the audience wasn't daunting enough, he had to then get his head around the fact that the extremely blunt Simon Cowell was sitting just a few feet from him.

"My name's Zayn," he told the panel. He then began to sing "Let Me Love You." He had practiced hard with this song and he felt confident that it was perfectly suited to his voice. On the stage, he gave it his all, and his rendition was enough to get him through to boot camp. Walsh said that he liked Zayn and Scherzinger said she felt he had something "special." Cowell was admiring, too, but added that he felt Zayn needed to become more ambitious. This was a fair criticism at this stage in their relationship.

In time, Cowell would appreciate that Zayn's somewhat placid exterior masks a very ambitious soul who wants success and all that comes with it. That ambition would not just surface, but grow, as Zayn continued in the contest. The most immediate hurdle for Zayn came with the voting. Walsh and Scherzinger both said "yes," and Zayn politely thanked them both. At this stage, with two positive votes, he was already through to boot camp as he had the majority in his favor. However, he bodly wanted to complete the set and get the much-prized nod from Cowell. He waited for Cowell to speak with anticipation. "Zayn, I'm going to say yes," said the head judge.

Louis Tomlinson was one of the last contestants to audition. There is a certain superstition surrounding the later auditions, as in season one of the British show *Pop Idol*—the eventual winner, Will Young, had been the very last singer to present himself to the judges. Some contestants believe that their chances increase the later in the process they audition. Like Zayn, Louis needed to leave for the audition at an unseemly hour—in Louis' case, he left for Manchester around midnight. His friend Stan went with him.

They slept in the car for a while when they arrived at the Manchester MEN Arena and lined up around 4 A.M. Contestants are willing to wait in line for many hours and at super early times in the morning. Critics of talent shows sometimes complain that fame is "handed out on a plate" by *The X Factor*. Yet how many who make this criticism could say that they have ever waited for hours, starting at a ridiculous time, for a job interview? Nobody can take Louis' dedication away from him.

He had quite a different look back on his audition day compared to the one he rocks nowadays. For starters, his hair was much longer. He has since described the lengthy, full-bodied mullet-like look he was sporting then as "pretty awful." Rather than wearing a striped T-shirt as he usually does in One Direction, he wore a shirt and tie with a baggy gray cardigan and blue jeans. In a sense, Louis' overall audition image fell somewhere between indie cool and boy-going-to-visit-his-grandma-to-ask-for-money. Yet, somehow, it worked.

After sleeping in line, only to be rudely awakened by a nudge from a fellow hopeful contestant, Louis found himself in the coldly named *X Factor* holding room. Time can move slowly in that room. Finally, a member of the production team appeared and called Louis' number. Suddenly, after all the waiting, everything seemed to be happening fast, and before he knew it he was waiting by the stage. Then, he was told it was time. As he walked onto the stage he was suddenly a little scared. He recalls that his "mouth went dry." The way he introduced himself, saying "My name's Louis Tomlinson," showed how nervous he was. His shy smile said it all. Not that his nerves were without advantage—the more shy he came across, the more adorable Louis became in the eyes of many.

The first song he sang was the Scouting For Girls song "Elvis Ain't Dead," a song that has become typical of the bouncy indie-pop sound of the band. However, before Louis could really get into his stride with the song he was stopped by Cowell, who felt that it would be better if Louis tried another song. For his second song, Louis had selected and rehearsed a much calmer one, "Hey There Delilah" by the Plain White T's. Although this choice would, in months to come, create a problem for Louis, on the day he auditioned it was enough to win the judges over. Scherzinger showed her approval even during the song, with a big smile on her face as she gently swayed along to the tune.

After Louis sang, Cowell and Walsh both said his voice was "interesting" and Scherzinger made a positive comment about his appearance. However, there was a general sense that they felt he was not confident enough. Although Louis has since attributed this to his exhaustion on that day, it is undoubtedly true that he found his confidence later in the competition. Then came the vote and, much like Niall's experience, it was hard for Louis to know what to expect. His namesake Walsh told him, "Louis—I'm saying yes." Scherzinger echoed this, exclaiming: "I'm saying yes." Could Louis complete the set with a positive from Cowell? He could. "You've got three yeses," said the head judge. Each member of the future band was safely through.

So, what can we learn about the band members from their auditions and their reactions to them? A recurring feature of the boys' recollections is a particularly pronounced desire to win the approval of Simon Cowell. There is nothing strange about this— many X Factor contestants admit that it is Cowell's verdict they await most anxiously. However, among the boys there is a sense that they see the head judge as a "family" figure, and to an extent, Simon Cowell reciprocates. He's not seen as a big brother but more as an "uncle" figure in the eyes of the band.

Things were looking good for the five boys but there were choppy waters ahead. By the end of the boot camp phase, they were cut from the competition, then reinstated as a band. It was definitely a roller-coaster ride for them. Before the highest of highs, the boys would taste the lowest of lows. "I met them as solo artists to begin with," Cowell later told *Rolling Stone* magazine. "Each of them individually had very good auditions. We had high hopes for two or three of them in particular, and then it all kind of fell apart at one of the latter stages."

It is worth stating at this point that there's an element of "legend building" behind the official narrative about what happened at boot camp. According to the story, the judges lost faith in each of the boys during the boot camp phase. Only after sending them home did the judges and producers consider that perhaps the boys could be formed into a band. It seems more likely that the decision to form a boy band was made a little earlier.

The boot camp phase was held at Wembley Arena and lasted five days in July 2010. A total of 211 contestants had made it through the auditions to this stage. From the first day of boot camp, on July 22, it was clear that boot camp would be just as brutal as in past seasons. Each of the four categories—boys, girls, over-25s, and groups—was given a different song to prepare. The boys—including the five future members of One Direction—were given Michael Jackson's "Man in the Mirror." This is an all-time pop classic and, as such, was regarded with reverence by the boys. (The other categories were also given tricky songs: the Girls were given "If I Were a Boy" by Beyoncé; the Groups got "Nothing's Gonna Stop Us Now" by Starship; while the over-25s got "Poker Face," the Lady Gaga hit.)

After the judges had gathered all the contestants, Simon Cowell told them what was at stake on day one of boot camp. "By the end of the day, half of you are going home," Cowell told them. "Today, you're going to be put in your categories and you're going to sing one song. There are literally no second chances." No wonder it was such a tense and difficult day. Compared to the opening auditions, during which contestants could sing any song of their choice, they were now feeling constrained creatively and under increasing pressure—which was exactly what the judges and production team wanted them to feel. Boot camp has never been about being fair or friendly—it is a survival-of-the-fittest, edge-of-your-seat ride. Each year there are shocks and surprises. Some contestants who had looked like finalists or even potential winners during auditions, would suddenly lose their "mojo" and were eliminated after poor performances. Likewise, some who only just made it through in the audition round would suddenly pluck new talent and charisma out of the bag.

It is not just the contestants that shock—so do the producers. There is often a "curve ball" surprise thrown in to add drama. In one season, a group of contestants was cut right at the beginning of boot camp. One can only imagine their hurt and disappointment as they realized they were being sent home before they had sung a solitary note, let alone a song. These twists are obviously designed to make dramatic television. For some viewers, though, they make for uncomfortable viewing. To watch people's dreams and emotions being toyed with feels cruel, to say the least.

In 2010, the first twist of boot camp was of a less brutal nature. However, for one future member of One Direction, it was still far from within his comfort zone. The five boys were ecstatic when their renditions of "Man in the Mirror" had been enough to get them through to the second day of boot camp. There was a ton of smiling, screaming, and cheering back in their hotel rooms that night. Their confidence and spirits were growing by the day. However, the spirits of one of them came crashing down the following day when the surviving contestants were told that the activity of the day would not be singing, but dancing.

Zayn was not alone in finding this a distinctly uncomfortable and unwelcome situation. Several contestants were unhappy to be dancing. Among them was Irish singer Mary Byrne. However, nobody reacted quite so extremely as Zayn. Choreographer Brian Friedman told them, "I don't want you to be scared—what we are going to work on is your stage presence and choreography." For Zayn, the reassurance came too late. He was miserable—he hated to dance. It was when this stage in the season was broadcast that viewers back home would be first introduced to him. He was shown telling a camera backstage, "I seriously don't want to do it because I hate dancing, and I've never done it before and I feel like an idiot on the stage with other people, who are clearly better than me … I'm not doing it!" With his discomfort growing, he added, "When you've got to perform in front of Simon and professionals that know what they're doing and how to dance, and professional choreographers and stuff, and I just don't know."

At this stage in the broadcast, Cowell seemed to notice Zayn's absence onstage. In truth, it's more likely that he had been tipped off about the problem by the producers. Cowell has struggled to remember the names of contestants even in the finals of the season, so the idea that he would notice the absence of one contestant on a packed stage seems unrealistic. In any case, this created more drama—the very thing the show thrives on. It also served as a useful way of introducing Zayn, whose initial audition had not been shown on-screen. Cowell was shown walking backstage to try and find the absent boy, having told Louis Walsh and

Brian Friedman to carry on their work while he found Zayn. When he did, he asked, "Zayn, why aren't you out there? You can't just bottle it, you can't just hide behind here! Zayn, you are ruining this for yourself. I'm trying to help you here. So, if you can't do it now, you're never going to be able to do it, right? Come on, let's go and do it!"

So they returned to the stage area. As Zayn was about to hop back onto the stage, Cowell made a final comment, half pep-talk, half warning. "Don't do that again, get on with it!" he told Zayn. They shook hands—and that was that. The first moment of management between Cowell and a member of One Direction had occurred. It would not be the last. Once Zayn began dancing it was clear why he had tried to avoid it, and Cowell described his efforts as "uncomfortable." For once, the dreaded judge was being kind instead of cutting. Dancing was clearly not Zayn's strong point. However, the fact that he had been brave enough to give something outside his comfort zone a try impressed Cowell and the producers. They would not want to put anyone who buckled under pressure into a band—so although Zayn didn't known it at the time, he had just passed his first test. "I'm glad that he did it—for himself," Cowell reflected afterward. The other four boys had done their best to dance well, but none had excelled. Cowell described Niall's efforts, for instance, as "all over the place."

The pressure was not going to abate any time soon—and it was not only Zayn who was feeling the pinch. As Harry reflected on-screen, the more hurdles he successfully negotiated, the greater and more intense his ambition became. It wasn't just feeling pleased to be there, or merely proud of what he had achieved thus far. Instead, he was gazing with fiery eyes at what could be achieved. He told the cameras, "As you go through boot camp, you kind of realize how big the prize is, so being here the last few days has made me realize how much I wanna stay—I really don't want to go home now."

The next twist of the season was one that only indirectly affected our boys, but is pertinent to understanding where they emerged from. Cheryl Cole was sent home after collapsing backstage, and it was later reported that she had contracted malaria while on vacation in Tanzania. She was taken to the hospital and told there would be a lengthy recuperation ahead of her. In Cheryl's absence, Cowell called in former Pussycat Dolls singer Nicole Scherzinger to take her place. (Ironically, this foreshadowed a drama that would erupt on *The X Factor* U.S. the following year when, after Cole was dropped as a judge, it was Scherzinger who moved from presenter duties to the judges' table.)

As a judge, Nicole Scherzinger was a familiar face to several of the boys because she was present at the initial auditions of a few of them, including Harry and Louis. With Dannii Minogue also absent, the judging panel was looking quite different. Another change was that the producers decided not to allow an audience to attend the process. The show's official Twitter account sent out the following message, "Due to the unusual circumstances, we are not inviting an audience to watch the contestants perform at *The X Factor* Boot Camp." This provided an added dose of drama to what happened next.

On the third day of boot camp, the contestants were handed a list of forty songs and told to choose one to sing. For some this was a gift. Unlike day one when they felt restricted, they now felt liberated. For others, though, this made life tougher—they simply could not decide which song to choose. As soon as they chose one, they would notice another song on the list that they liked. When they could have been working hard on perfecting their chosen song, they were instead wasting time with all of this indecisiveness. This was the final hurdle before judges' houses—a terrible time to be unfocused. Once it was their time to sing, they would take to the stage individually, perform, and then leave. The judges would not be giving them any feedback at the time of the performance.

Liam chose to sing "Stop Crying Your Eyes Out" by Oasis. It was not a difficult choice for him. As we have seen, he loves Oasis and had sung their songs since he was a little kid, adopting the famous Liam Gallagher posture. Before he went on stage, he explained on camera what was at stake for him. He described his successful first audition as "a brilliant bonus—my feet still haven't touched the floor." He then said that there was also "a negative" about it, "because I've got to try and live up to it." Having had a year to prepare for his opening audition, he had just twenty-four hours to get ready for his next one. He was shown making a mistake during rehearsals, and Brian Friedman said that this was due to "his age." Again, for Liam the moment was to be all about pleasing Cowell. "I want to prove to Simon that I'm here and I mean business," he said. "I want to show him that I've got what it takes."

He walked onstage with grace and confidence. "Hi everybody. How are you doing, judges?" he asked, casually. Before singing, he was invited to explain why he felt he had the "X factor." With his right leg shuffling with nerves, Liam said he felt he had it, "because I had a knock-back at an early age—I took on a huge challenge, set myself a goal and I never gave up." As in past appearances in front of Cowell, Liam had pitched himself well.

Then he sang the Oasis song. This was a performance that divided viewers—some felt it was a bit stale and boring, many felt it was an emotional and convincing rendition. Certainly, it lacked some of the drama of his "Cry Me a River" audition, but as Liam had noted, that was always going to be a tough one to live up to. Liam was beginning to inject some more oomph into it when Cowell cut him off. With that, it was time for him to leave and let the judges discuss his prospects without him present. "Oh, Simon, he's good," whispered Walsh after Liam had left the stage. "I like him. Simon, girls are going to like him," added the Irishman. Cowell's body language showed he was not convinced. "I like him, but I think he's a little bit one dimensional," he said. Walsh continued to put Liam's case. "He's a young pub singer, Simon," he said. "And he's only sixteen."

Later, Cowell showed that he was less than convinced. Speaking on the sister show *The Xtra Factor*, he said, "The world we live in today, compared to a year ago, is that you have to stand out from the rest. So someone like Liam is an example of who, maybe a year or two years ago, I would have thought of as a good contestant on this show. But now he just bores the pants off me." Expanding on his theme, he said, "When there's a ceiling on somebody's talent, which there is with Liam, you can only take him so far, so you're always limited by that. When you're working with someone, that's frustrating, because you want to feel that you can throw anything at them and they'll cope with it or make it better." None of this painted a rosy future for Liam.

Once he and the other four boys—whose day-three songs were not broadcast—had performed, it was time for the judges to confer. Due to the continued absence of Minogue and Cole, a few changes were made to the format. Instead of putting six acts through in each category, Cowell, Walsh and Scherzinger agreed to send eight acts to each judges' house. This partly reflected their confidence that there were many acts worthy of progression and partly allowed Minogue and Cole the chance to have a wider variety of acts to choose from. A change was also made to the category age divisions. At Scherzinger's suggestion, the over-25s were changed to the over-28s.

When the thirty remaining boys—including Harry, Liam, Louis, Niall, and Zayn—were called to the stage, they could hardly have been more anxious. Zayn arrived nervously rubbing his hands together. Liam looked like he wanted to faint—or cry. Then the judges began to announce the names of those who had got through. Cowell started by naming John Wilding, then Scherzinger announced Nicolo Festa's name. As more and more names were announced, the boys became more nervous and scared. It was notable, though, that Louis made a point of clapping and smiling politely to acknowledge the joy of each contestant who had been lucky enough to have their name announced. He even patted Karl Brown on the back as he got the nod. His grace made the knowledge of the disappointment he was feeling all the more heartbreaking for the viewers.

Eventually, there were two more names to be announced. Each of the five boys hoped that his would be one of them, while also despairing that this was going to be the case. The final two names called out were those of Matt Cardle, the eventual winner, and Tom Richards. "That's it, guys—I'm really sorry," said Cowell. As Richards left the stage in tears of joy, the contestants remaining onstage tried to come to terms with the fact that they were out. Liam, who had been rejected at this stage in 2008, only to be reinstated minutes later, shuffled uncomfortably from foot to foot as he faced the reality of elimination. He held his hand to his head and fought tears. The tears won the battle. Harry looked out in shock and Niall ruffled his own hair, a look of desperation and heartbreak etched into his face.

When Liam left the stage he was given a commiserating hug by Dermot O'Leary. "I just don't want to go home," he said, barely audibly. "I just don't want to go." Then Harry spoke. Though he seemed to be handling it marginally better than Liam, he was, he explained, "really gutted" and he looked it. Niall, meanwhile, was more animated, though a sense of anger seemed present amid his heartbreak. "Worst thing I've ever felt in my life," he said. "Standing there, waiting for your name to be called, and then it's not." As tears returned to his eyes he apologized to the interviewer and walked away, covering his face with his shirt.

However, Cowell was not happy to lose the boys. "I had a bad feeling that maybe we shouldn't have lost them and maybe there was something else we should do with them," he explained later in an interview with *Rolling Stone*. "And this is when the idea came about that we should see if they could work as a group." Whether the decision was made on the spur of that moment or had been a more premeditated option, it was now time to act on it. A boy band and a girl band—to be named Belle Amie—would be formed out of some of the rejected contestants. Backstage, the production team gathered Louis, Liam, Harry, Niall, and Zayn together. They also called back the four girls, who would be formed into Belle Amie.

At this stage none of them knew what was in store. For Liam, this was a particularly surreal moment. Just as in 2008, he had been told he was going home only to be recalled minutes later. As they were led back to the stage, more than one of the boys and girls were anxiously biting their fingernails. The boys lined up on the stage. Their faces and body language said it all: they were downcast to have been beaten by the competition, confused as to why they had been called back, and simultaneously trying to keep a lid on their expectations. Meanwhile, the judges looked at the two groups and wondered silently to themselves whether they had made the right decision. As Cowell looked at the five boys, he had no doubt. "The minute they stood there for the first time together—it was a weird feeling," he told *Rolling Stone* later. "They just looked like a group at that point." There is something touching, almost eerie, about the way the five boys melded into a single unit in that moment.

It was Scherzinger who kicked-off the explanation. "Hello, thank you so much for coming back," she told them. "Judging from some of your faces, this is really hard. We've thought long and hard about it and we've thought of each of you as individuals and we just feel that you're too talented to let go of. We think it would be a great idea to have two separate groups." Still, the penny had not completely dropped with the contestants, so Cowell decided to make it clear. "We've decided to put you both through to the judges' houses," he told them. The five boys erupted with joy—Louis leapt like a kangaroo, while Harry sank to his knees. The judges looked on with happiness as they witnessed the relief and excitement. Then Cowell decided it was time to give them a reality check. "Guys, guys, girls, girls— this is a lifeline—you've got to work ten, twelve, fourteen hours a day, every single day, and take this opportunity," he told them. "You've got a real shot here, guys."

The boys bounced off the stage feeling like they had just won the World Cup. Harry spoke for all five when he told O'Leary, "I went from the worst feeling in my life to the best." Then it was time for them to be reunited with the other contestants who had made it through earlier. They ran into each other's arms and embraced. Life felt really good. However, there was one more obstacle for the boys to overcome.

They were asked to make absolutely sure that they were happy to be formed into a band. After all, each had auditioned very much as a solo artist. Nobody wanted a band containing a member whose heart was not in the idea of performing as a unit, so it was a sensible decision to encourage each boy to search his soul. It was Liam who took time to make up his mind. Since his 2008 *X Factor* experience, he had worked hard to build the beginnings of a solo career. At first, he felt it was unimaginable to leave all that work behind and instead join a band. He searched his soul, took advice from those he respected and trusted most, and then came to a clear decision—he was in. It was in that very moment that the band was officially formed.

The next milestone came when the judges were informed what category they would be mentoring for the remainder of the season. The production team called each judge with the news, and Simon Cowell was told he would be given the groups. Traditionally, the groups are seen as one of the two weaker categories—along with the elder solo category. Although he knew that One Direction was a strong prospect, Cowell played up to the script by sarcastically responding to the news, saying, "Thank you for repaying all of my hard work on the show this year." As this episode was broadcast, *X Factor* viewers lapped up the drama surrounding the formation of One Direction and Belle Amie. Among the viewers were the band members and their families. Louis' mother, Johannah, told the local press, "We had a family party to watch the boot camp stages of the show on Sunday and we were all so proud of Louis and the boys. He's so excited; he can't quite believe he has made it this far."

For the judges' houses phase of the show, the band flew to Marbella in Spain to perform in front of Cowell. For the successful acts in this stage of the process, the prize is huge—a place in the live shows. For the unsuccessful acts, the disappointment is just as strong. As Liam knew, and any athlete will tell you, losing a semi-final is worse than losing a final. For *X Factor* contestants, much the same is true of the judges' houses, which is, in effect, the semifinal stage. The boys were nervous and excited—Zayn particularly so, because this was his first trip abroad and he had to apply for a passport just for the trip. Boys will be boys, so there were some fun moments in Marbella—though the tabloid reports of Cowell's house being trashed were colorfully exaggerated. However, they did have time to sit by the beach. Louis and Zayn fondly remember sitting together eating pizza, looking out into the sea. Aside from the good times, they were there to work and were determined to succeed.

They did not so much convince Cowell of their talent, as blow him away. Speaking later to *Rolling Stone* magazine about the band's history, Cowell was asked when he first realized that the band could be huge. "When they came to my house in Spain and performed, after about a millionth of a second," he said. "I tried to keep a straight face for a bit of drama for the show."

For their performance, the boys sang "Torn," originally a hit for Australian singer Natalie Imbruglia, who had been a guest judge at Liam's audition earlier in the season. But there was drama before the audition when Louis was stung by a sea urchin while the boys swam in the ocean. At first, he assumed he had cut his foot on a sharp stone or a piece of glass. However, when he woke the next morning he was horrified to discover that his foot had swollen to twice its normal size. When he got out of bed he immediately fell over. He called for help and was taken to the hospital, where he was given an injection. The shock of the pain from the needle was so intense that poor Louis reportedly threw up.

Meanwhile, the rest of the band waited anxiously to see if he would be able to perform. When they saw him arrive back from the hospital, they were so thrilled that they ran and smothered him with hugs and then lifted him between them and carried him along to their performance. Cowell quickly noticed Louis' slight limp when they arrived to sing. Louis assured the judge that he was fine. Then they sang. Liam led the vocals during the first verse, Harry took the bridge, and then all five sang during the chorus. As they swung their hips during the final chorus, the band suddenly looked surprisingly convincing as a unit, considering the tender age of both the band itself and its individuals.

At the end of the song, Cowell gave nothing away to the band, merely saying, "See you later." However, as the boys filed away from the audition, Cowell was struggling to contain his enthusiasm. He and his assistant Sinitta both expressed their excitement over what they had seen. "The second they left I jumped out of my chair," he recalled in *Rolling Stone*. "They just had it. They had this confidence. They were fun. They worked out the arrangements themselves. They were like a gang of friends, and kind of fearless as well." There would be little soul-searching needed when he decided whether to put One Direction through to the live shows.

Still, when it came to breaking the news to them the following day, Cowell naturally played it as deadpan as he could while building their and the viewers' suspense. "My head is saying it's a risk and my heart is saying that you deserve a shot," he told them. The boys stood waiting, practically breathless with anxiety. Liam was particularly tense—he did not want to go home at this stage for the second time. "And that's why it's been difficult. So I've made a decision. Guys, I've gone with my heart—you're through!"

The roar that came from the boys as they celebrated said it all. They then ran to celebrate with Cowell—Harry the first to arrive in the arms of their mentor. "I am so impressed with all of you, I mean that," Cowell told them. Four of the newly confirmed finalists then jumped fully clothed into the nearby swimming pool. "We went crazy," remembered Liam. Louis, still under the weather from the sting, decided not to join them in the water.

On the plane home to England, the band members were in high spirits. They had made it through to the live shows and would soon be singing in front of the nation. It was, to use the phrase at the start of each *X Factor* live show, time . . . to face . . . the music!

7 GOING LIVE!

In truth, the scariest thing that contestants face in the live shows is not "the music," or even the judges. Instead, it is the public vote. The live shows are an exciting experience for all contestants. Not only do they perform to a live studio audience and a primetime TV audience of millions, they also face weekly feedback from each of the four judges. Having successfully dealt with all of that, they then face the public vote. The phone lines are open for twenty-four hours after the performance, and the bottom two acts then face a "sing-off," before the judges decide which of the two will be sent home. As they prepared for the first weekend, the boys were just hoping to make it through to week two. They didn't know at the time that they had ten weeks of live shows ahead of them,—and that they were on their way to the final show.

Each week, the judges provided their opinions and advice after the performances. Although the feedback was mostly positive, each judge had his/her individual quirks, with which the boys would become more familiar as time progressed. For instance, Louis Walsh habitually deemed them "the next big boy band."

Dannii Minogue, though, was the most constructive on the panel. She was never harsh, and her observations were fair, accurate, and aimed at getting the best out of the band. She was the most honest and the least caught-up with One Direction mania. Cheryl Cole, meanwhile, made amusing admissions of a growing One Direction fandom. Cowell was his usual confident self. As the band's mentor, not to mention the king of the *X Factor* universe, he sat with broad shoulders—both literally and metaphorically—as his young prodigies sailed through, week by week. Let's start at the beginning . . .

(*From top, left to right*) Five solo acts Niall, Harry, Louis, Liam, and Zayn become a band— One Direction is born.

The boys bonded quickly and it was not long before they developed a style of their own.

Above: Dazzled by fans and posing with mentor Simon Cowell who would lead the boys to the final.

Below: Nicky Byrne and Shane Filan from Westlife offer the boys their support.

Above: The boys were amazed at the crowds of cheering fans.

Below: Onstage at Louis' old school in Doncaster, England during the final stages of the competition.

Above: Which one's which? You can bet all their fans know.

Below: Isn't he cute? Harry holds up a childhood photo on a visit to his hometown.

Above: Born to do it, the boys strike a pose on the red carpet at the premiere of *The Chronicles of Narnia: The Voyage of the Dawn Treader.*

Below: Working their magic at the world premiere of *Harry Potter and the Deathly Hallows: Part 1.*

Above: At an *X Factor* press conference before the final, the boys look relaxed and confident.

Below: With fellow contestants of season seven, including eventual winner Matt Cardle.

Above: The roller-coaster ride begins: the boys perform in the *X Factor* live tour.

Left: The band becomes the face of Pokémon.

Week One
Theme: Number ones

In the first week, the band sang "Viva La Vida" by Coldplay. It was a song choice that took many viewers by surprise. A bold statement was being made early on—this was not going to be just another cookie cutter boy band. It might have been tempting to hand them a Westlife ballad, a Take That anthem, or a song by The Wanted. Instead, they were given a Coldplay song. "You wouldn't actually connect this band normally with this song—but strangely, it works," said Cowell, during the introductory, personalized video that is aired immediately prior to each contestant's performance. Zayn explained he was worried he might miss his cue. He felt quite overwhelmed by the length and intensity of the build-up to the first live show.

As the drama of the video built, Cole said, "These guys really need to step up and deliver—there's a lot of pressure!" The band stood waiting for the doors at the back of the stage to open. Beyond those doors were the studio audience, judges, and the cameras that would transport them into the living rooms of millions. Harry was so nervous that he got sick. However, the band had, Louis explained, made sure they focused on their own song, rather than worrying about the competition. It was a wise approach, and now came the time to deliver.

As the band appeared and sang the song, each boy showed a different emotion. Liam, at the center of it all, looked masterful and poised. His extensive experience with live performances on television was clear. Late in the song when the performance wilted slightly, it was Liam who burst into action—urging the other band members to up their games. Harry, meanwhile, showed his nerves with an intense, almost aggressive stage presence. As he thumped his shoulder to the beat, his facial expression tried, unsuccessfully, to conceal his nerves. Zayn, as had been anticipated, did look concerned in the seconds before his cue, but after successfully meeting it, he began to look happier as he got into his groove.

Which leaves us with Louis and Niall. Mr. Tomlinson looked excited to be there, more or less relaxed onstage and with his usual sense of fun. Perhaps the combination of being the oldest member of the group and having comparatively lesser responsibilities during the song helped to keep him relaxed. Niall, meanwhile, managed to smile the whole way through the performance. Even as he sang his part, the lyrics dealing with regret and disappointment, he continued to smile. The incongruity of this was forgivable under the circumstances—it was just nice to see someone enjoying himself so much.

As the band moved into position for Liam's solo, concluding line, they were already smiling with excitement and satisfaction that they got through the song so well. At the end, they embraced each other, much like a group of boys at the end of a soccer game. It was these moments that reminded viewers what they were watching—a band of young boys at the very start of their career. This made them all the more impressive and enchanting because it gave them an "underdog" identity—all the better to attract the public vote.

The panel applauded, and Cowell smiled with pride. Louis told them, "Wow guys, when I heard you were going to do Coldplay I thought it was a big, big risk! I love what you did with the song— you totally made it your own. I love that the band is gelling, even though Simon's going to claim he put this band together—it was my idea originally, Simon. It was! Boys, I think potentially you could be the next big boy band, but you have a lot of work to do." He added, with a sting, "But Simon Cowell, I'm not sure about the styling! Did you have a stylist?" As the audience indulged in some theatrical booing, Walsh hardened his face and jutted out his chin.

Dannii Minogue spoke next. "Guys, I don't know whose idea it was because I wasn't there, but you look like you fit together, you're the perfect band," she said. The boys were so thrilled with the feedback, that their enthusiasm was infectious. "That song was fantastic and you did make it your own," added the Australian. Cheryl Cole felt the same way. "I have to agree with Dannii, you look like you were meant to be together as a group," she said, to the continued delight of One Direction. "I reckon the girls will be going crazy for you, but you need a little bit more time to develop as a group, that's all. Just a little bit more time."

Their mentor then chipped in. "Regarding your role in putting the group together, Louis, we'll rewind the tapes on that one," said Cowell. Walsh defiantly told him he should. "You guys came together because your boot camp auditions weren't good enough but you were too good to throw away," Cowell continued. "We took a risk, and I've got to tell you, what was so impressive about that was when you started to screw up—one of you at the end, Liam stepped in, you brought it back together. That's what bands do." He then turned to Walsh's comments regarding styling, "Louis, I don't want to style a band like this. We asked the band to do whatever they wanted to do—I'm not going to interfere, they're going to do it their way. It was brilliant, guys."

Onstage, Dermot O'Leary joined the conversation, saying, "Louis, with the greatest respect, how do you know what eighteen-year-olds should be wearing? Come on, man!" Harry stood aside from all the bickering and summed up what the band was thinking, "It was the best experience of all of our lives," he said. Zayn later reflected that each band member was "buzzing" as they left the stage. Each one just had their largest dose of "performance high."

The following night they nervously awaited their fate as the public vote was announced. After the show had ended, Liam said that waiting for the results of the first week's public vote was the one time that made them the most nervous. Luckily, they survived the vote to go through to week two. Less lucky was Nicolo Festa, who left automatically after finishing last, and FYD, who lost the sing-off against Katie Waissel.

Meanwhile, Cowell had noticed something very special about One Direction—they were quickly attracting huge gatherings of fans outside the studio. "It was unusual because, in an instant, we had hundreds of fans outside the studio," he would later tell *Rolling Stone*. "That doesn't happen very often." Expanding on the exchange he had with Walsh over the band's styling, he explained, "They had good taste and they understood the kind of group they wanted to be. They didn't want to be molded. I'm not interested in working with people like that either."

Week Two
Theme: Heroes

In the second week of the live shows, fourteen acts still remained. This figure was itself a reminder to One Direction and their fellow contestants of the scale of the challenge—even having lost two acts in week one, there were still thirteen other acts to get voted off before a winner would be crowned. They would all have to work hard. It was a tough week for the band because Harry had another attack of nerves during the sound check. He could not breathe properly and felt like he was going to be sick again. It is remarkable to reflect that Harry, who is now the central and oftentimes effortlessly confident figure of the band, was the one who struggled most with the pressure early on. It was a surprise to him, too, as he had never before been so hit by nerves that his ability to perform was called into question.

Their song for this week was "My Life Would Suck Without You," by Kelly Clarkson. There was a nice symbolism behind the song choice—Clarkson, who won the first season of *American Idol*, is one of the most successful graduates of television talent show history. However, musically, as a female solo artist's song, it was again an unlikely choice. Even still, the band performed it well. As Liam took the opening verse, the camera panned between the others. It immediately showed Niall and Louis grinning again, while Harry was again moving along to the music. Zayn? He looked serious and sultry. By the end of the song, the relief and joy of all members was palpable. So Zayn might have delivered one less than perfect note—the important thing was that they had basically nailed it. Louis offered the nervous Harry a protective hug.

Walsh was the first to speak. "Well, One Direction, you seem to be having fun on stage," he said. "Every schoolgirl up and down the country is going to love this. My only problem, boys, is with your mentor, Simon. Kelly Clarkson a hero? Simon, why? It was a strange song. Boys, you are really, really good but I think Simon Cowell could've picked a better song." As the boos rang out, Dannii Minogue said, "Boys, maybe that's your musical hero. I have to say that you're five heartthrobs. You look great together and Harry, whatever nerves you have, I'm sure your friends and you will stick together. The true measure of a boy band like you will be when you sing your big ballad, so I will be looking forward to hearing that." The band appreciated her feedback—they were dying to sing a ballad.

"I can't even cope with how cute you are. Seriously, I can't!" said Cheryl Cole. Harry put his hands together in a praying motion, his prayers had just been answered. "I just want to go over and hug them, in a nice way. You're so sweet, I'm watching you the whole time just thinking, 'This is adorable!'" All the while, Cowell comically warned her off the boys, saying, "No, no, no!" When it came to his time to judge, he offered the band some colossal praise. "Let me tell you, you are the most exciting pop band in the country today," he told the boys, much to their shock and awe. Liam in particular looked stunned by the statement. "I'm being serious—there is something absolutely right." Cowell has never been one to measure his remarks—performances tend to be the best or worst he has ever seen. Nobody in the studio was letting that get in the way of their excitement, though. As the audience cheered Cowell's words, Harry theatrically urged them to cheer louder. There was even louder cheering and celebrations galore when One Direction were again sent through by the public vote.

Week Three
Theme: Guilty pleasures

The boys recounted the crazy experience they and the other remaining finalists had during a high-profile shopping trip in the build-up to week three. It was their first encounter with the hysteria that was growing among their increasing fan base. As they arrived, the screams from the girls were deafening. In years to come, this would seem like a small-fry encounter for the band, but at the time it was almost terrifyingly intense. "He winked at me, he winked at me, he winked at me!" screamed one of the girls, convinced she had "had a moment" with one of the band members. Louis recalled how they were "absolutely mobbed by teenage girls, which is all right!" So, too, were the free clothes they were allowed to pick up during the trip.

Returning to the music, Cowell explained how

during the week he changed the song that the band would sing. As usual with *The X Factor*, such a decision was hyped and dramatized for the show. It was presented as a challenge that, in the words of Dannii Minogue, many performers would not be able to overcome. The band was given that invaluable identity for a talent show—the underdog.

The new song was "Nobody Knows" by Pink. With a slightly more somber tune, the band—even Louis and Niall—looked more serious and soulful than in previous weeks. This was the closest that One Direction came to the boy band standard—the ballad. At the climax of the song, the producers even deployed pyrotechnics behind them. Louis could not resist turning to look at them as they went off.

Perhaps the more significant aspect of this performance was that Harry had some solos throughout. While Liam was still the lead member, Harry's confidence was rising and, with it, so was his place within One Direction. Walsh paid tribute to Liam's lead in his feedback. "You just have to walk out on the stage—everybody's screaming," said the Irishman. "It's like five Justin Biebers! And Liam— brilliant lead vocal from you!" Minogue observed that they were "living the dream." Cole, though, stole the night with her comment, which had the audience and band enraptured, "You know what, guys?" she asked, "Let me just put this out there—you are my guilty pleasure!" Praise from the gorgeous Cole—that was, right there, irrefutable evidence that the band was in fact living the dream. Cole added, "Whenever The Beatles went anywhere, they caused that level of hysteria. You're finding your feet now; I'm looking forward to seeing you improve even more."

Cowell was his usual proud self. Having milked the whole song change issue as much as he could, he said, "I've got to tell you, apart from it being a great performance, I thought vocally, you've really, really made some really huge improvements." Backstage after they had performed, Harry spoke with excitement about another week of praise from the judges. "The comments were absolutely brilliant," he beamed. "For us to keep proceeding in the competition, we have to get better every week."

In keeping with the spirit of the week, the band was asked what their top three choices would be as guilty pleasure songs. They revealed that their ultimate guilty pleasure song was John Travolta singing "Greased Lightning." Behind that was "Tease Me" by Chaka Demus & Pliers, and in third place was that infuriatingly catchy, cheesy pop hit "I'm Too Sexy" by Right Said Fred.

For their growing fan base, One Direction was not a guilty, but a proud, pleasure. Girls across the country were screaming with love for the new boy band. As for the boys themselves, they sailed into week three after the public vote was announced. They had seen judge Cole perform live during the weekend shows. This iconic fame that she enjoyed was just what they had wanted from the day they first applied to the show. Now, having survived the dreaded bottom two for two successive weeks, their confidence was really growing. Though they tried to keep their feet on the ground, they began to dare to believe. It was game on.

Week Four
Theme: Halloween

The themes for the live shows of *The X Factor* are sometimes unimaginative, but for the third week of the season, the "Halloween" theme promised more fun than usual. During the intervening week, the contestants visited the London Dungeon and Niall, in particular, was quite freaked out by the experience. On Saturday night, with songs such as Michael Jackson's "Thriller," "Bat Out of Hell" by Meatloaf, and "Bewitched" by Steve Lawrence among those that were sung, and with scary sets including vampires and witches, it made for a ghoulish evening. One Direction sang the Bonnie Tyler hit "Total Eclipse of the Heart." Since this is covered by the band Westlife, this was much more of a boy band song.

Done up in ghostly, vampiric make-up, the boys looked the part, on a stage laced with dry ice. Although Harry stood in the center of the line-up, it was Liam who again led the vocals. Niall popped in with some back-up lines, and Zayn leant his suitably smoky voice, too. The audience's applause at the end of the song was notably louder and longer than for any of the other performances that evening. As they listened to the acclaim, the band stood with more pride and comfort than ever before.

"I love the whole *Twilight*, vampire thing going on in the background," said Walsh, leading the judges' feedback. "Simon, it's definitely working." The fact that Walsh didn't tease Cowell about his boy band proved how One Direction had become more of a prospect. Minogue added, "You make vampire hot—I want to come to your party!" As for Cole, she too spoke with excitement at the band's commercial potential, "It doesn't matter where I go, somebody, an older woman, young women, kids—everybody mentions One Direction. I think you have a really long way to go in this competition."

It was left to their proud mentor to sum up the band's performance. "What I really admire about you guys," began Cowell, "is I know people are under pressure when you go into a competition like this. You've got to remember, you're sixteen, seventeen years old. The way you've conducted yourselves— don't believe the hype . . . work hard, rehearse. Honestly, it's a total pleasure working with you lot." Dermot O'Leary summed-up the atmosphere when he said, simply, "Wow!" On the following night's show, Harry said, "Last night felt brilliant. We got a real chance to show off our vocals and hopefully the fans at home will vote and keep us in because we really don't want to go home now."

The fans at home voted. The band was through to fight another week.

Week Five
Theme: American anthems

If there was a week when One Direction truly stamped their authority on the competition, it was in week five. They were given the final spot—the dream spot—of the night, much prized because it means you perform just minutes before the lines open for the public to vote. With your hopefully climactic performance fresh in the viewers' minds, you have a good chance of attracting a lot of votes. "You know what they say about saving the best till last," said Cowell, introducing them with that smile of his that combines a touch of pride with a dash of sarcasm. It was clear that Cowell believed there was something special to come.

There certainly was. Following an introductory clip that showed the boys messing around in the contestants' house—including some gratuitous scenes of Harry and Zayn in just their underwear—they appeared on the stage to sing the Kim Wilde hit, "Kids in America." Wearing colorful outfits, including classic American baseball jackets, and with cheerleaders behind them, the boys looked just like a band from the other side of the Atlantic. They would have fit right in on a Disney television series, or even *High School Musical*. They moved off the stage at one point, singing on the raised platform behind the judges, taking them just inches away from the screaming audience.

It was a performance of great authority. The way Harry leapt up at the end of the song, landing with a defiant thump on the final note, summed up their confidence. Walsh told the band how far they had already come. "Listen, everywhere I go there's hysteria, it's building on this band," he said. "You remind me a bit of Westlife, Take That, Boyzone . . . you could be the next big band." Minogue stepped out of the aforementioned hysteria to offer a more constructive judgment. "I don't think, vocally, it was the best of the night but a great performance," she said. Cole told One Direction, "That absolutely cheered me up and brightened up my night; I thoroughly enjoyed that performance. You are great kids—I love chatting to you backstage." Then, proud old Uncle Simon declared, "That was, without question, your best performance by a mile."

The future suddenly looked bright, though a shadow was cast when some viewers accused the band of lip syncing during their rendition of the Kim Wilde song. They pointed out that at one point in the song, Zayn looked as if he had missed his cue, yet his voice was audible before he lifted the microphone to his mouth. Twitter quickly surged with accusations, and former *X Factor* winner Shayne Ward was quoted in the *Sun* newspaper, attacking the band for lip syncing. This controversy was not what the band wanted to be reading. It seemed like yesterday that they were five ordinary teenage boys. Now, they were facing their first "media storm." Their defense was that Zayn did miss his cue, but it was not his voice that was heard—it was Harry's. With the camera focusing on Zayn, it was easy for viewers to confuse this. The explanation partially placated their online critics. Ward quickly distanced himself from his allegations, saying the journalist had twisted his words.

When the results were announced on the Sunday evening show, the band was relieved to learn that they had once again survived the public vote. The lip syncing controversy hit them hard at the time, but it also offered them a valuable lesson in the realities of fame and success. They realized that, while they had a huge, dedicated, and growing fan base, they also faced non-stop scrutiny from those who were less enamored of them. The live shows were proving to be a crash-course in fame for One Direction.

Week Six
Theme: Elton John

Elton John's music is, obviously, composed with a solo performer in mind. As the last band standing in the season, One Direction had to choose carefully the song they would pick from his vast and stately catalog. They went with "Something About the Way

You Look Tonight." They had the second to last spot of the night. Harry, standing in the center of the line-up, contributed his most significant solo of the season to date. The show's producers had noted the growing frenzy around him and, with his poise growing week by week, were moving him to a more leading role in the band. As he began his first line, the screams and howls from the audience showed that this was a popular move.

Cowell gave the band a standing ovation at the end and, throughout his fellow judges' commentary, encouraged the audience to cheer louder. Walsh told the boys, "Well, boys, after that performance I think you're only going in one direction, and that direction is the final. I talked to you guys a lot yesterday and I really got to know you. I know that you're taking the whole thing really, really serious and you know, you're going to be the next big boy band." Dannii Minogue added, "Guys, you are so consistent, it's scary!" Cheryl Cole, hearing the huge and frenzied cheer from the studio audience, said, "Listen to that! That's what it's all about; to hear that is the measure of what you've become."

Finally, Simon Cowell said, "Guys, I want to say

something, okay? This is the first time in all the years of *X Factor* where I genuinely believe a group is going to win this competition." He then reflected on their courteous and professional personalities, before concluding, "Guys, congratulations."

Everything was blooming in the world of One Direction. The season had taken a gamble by forming the band in front of the viewers' eyes, yet it was a gamble that was paying off. Each week, their stature and popularity was growing. Louis, talking about their Elton evening, said, "Last night was absolutely incredible, the crowd was amazing." Zayn assessed how the challenge was adapting week by week, and reflected that, "the competition's really, really heating up." It really was—and the growing army of fans felt that the hottest act of all was One Direction.

Week Seven
Theme: The Beatles

At last—a genre that fit a boy band best! Surrounded by male and female solo artists, One Direction had endured weekly themes that were not really in their comfort zone. However, The Beatles week was right up their alley. This was particularly true of Liam, who told the official *X Factor* website, "I'm a massive fan of The Beatles and I'm really looking forward to tonight." He previewed a "complicated performance," which would be "full of harmonies and ad libs, but it's the sort of performance that I think you'd expect from a top boy band."

They sang an up-tempo version of "All You Need Is Love." Harry again took plenty of the vocals, and what had started as a quiet performance ended in rapture, with dancers behind the band bouncing up and down. It was not, though, without its imperfections. "Thank God for you guys," said Walsh in his feedback, adding that, "it is good to see the Fab Five singing the Fab Four." Minogue, though, gave a touch of criticism. "I've always given you good comments," she began, "I just have to say tonight, you guys [Zayn and Niall] were struggling. I don't know if it was caught on-camera, but you were struggling with the backing vocals. Don't let the other guys down, you have to work as a group." Cowell, when it came to his turn, gestured to his three fellow judges, and said, "They do not want you to do well in the competition. I do—please vote!"

Afterward, Niall took Minogue's criticism lightly. "[She] gave us a bad comment but we're going to get bad comments," he said. "So we've got to take it on board and improve it next week." Niall showed that the cocky boy who auditioned in Dublin was already maturing into a more intelligent and poised personality.

Week Eight
Theme: Rock

This was the week that Harry's ascendancy within the band neared its peak. Although Liam still took plenty of the vocals for their opening lines of the two-song night, the very choice of song was Harry's. They sang "Summer of '69," a song Harry had sung as a boy. With the song choice presented on-air as entirely Harry's doing, he was getting plenty of attention. Already, it had been reported that Harry had come up with the name of the band, after commenting that they were all "headed in one direction." He also led the band on their mid-song tour and as they returned to the stage, it was Harry who was positioned in the center for the song's conclusion. It was as if a musical changing of the guard was occurring. Walsh told them, "Hey, boys—it absolutely worked! I love the choice of song, I love the vibe, the vitality you bring to the competition. The competition would not be the same without One Direction." Amen to that, thought a nation of young female viewers. Minogue was more positive than the previous week, saying, "You've clearly done lots of work and really stepped it up; I like that." Cole was stunned by the audience hysteria, saying, "We've got feet stamping going on, there's electricity in the room, it's fantastic."

However, it was Cowell whose comments were most significant. "I had nothing to do with this song choice—Harry chose the song, great choice of song," he said. As Harry beamed his winning smile he was congratulated by his band mates, with Niall even toying with Harry's famous curly locks. With the semi-final looming the following week, Cowell reminded the boys—but essentially the audience— that they had "worked your butts off to get where you've got," and implored the audience once more to "Please—pick up the phone!"

It should have been good times for the band. Everyone looked happy again—except for one member. Liam, perhaps feeling relegated by the attention and increasing prominence of Harry, was notably sad as O'Leary continued the Harry love-fest. As O'Leary read out the number for viewers to call to vote for One Direction, Liam was the only member not smiling. He toyed with his microphone at one point, but he was otherwise detached.

For the second song, they sang "You Are So Beautiful." It was difficult to argue with the producers' decision to increasingly focus on Harry, as he tenderly sang his lines, the camera zooming close on his boyish face, his eyes the definition of boy band dolefulness. Walsh told them that the song had proven that they are "a great vocal group—everyone in this group can sing." Minogue told them they were "stunning" and Cole added that she felt they had "a really bright future." Cowell told them, "In many ways that was my favorite performance from you," and singled Zayn out for praise.

The public voted for them again in sufficient numbers to put them straight through. They were in the semifinals!

The Semifinal

Their first song was a twist on Rihanna's monster hit "Only Girl (in the World)." By this stage in the competition, the band had become so polished that they no longer took to the stage as the freshly formed underdogs, unable to believe their luck. Instead, they carried themselves as an established band—with all the confidence that this entails. As they promised to make the subject of the song the only girl in the world, girls across the nation wished that they were that girl. Walsh told them, "Week after week, you're getting better and better, and you bring hysteria to the show. If there is any justice you will absolutely be in the final—you deserve to be in the final." Minogue was again less flattering with her comment. "Guys, I hope you never let us down because I really wanna see you guys as the next big boy band," she began. Taking her role as a judge seriously, she then offered some constructive criticism, telling them, "I have to say, some weeks you come out and I think it's very dull. That one was brilliant—you really stepped it up for the semifinals."

Cole then spoke about her part in the band's

week, during which she had effectively stood in for Cowell, who had been absent. "This week, for me, I got to know you all a little bit better because your mentor wasn't here," she said. "I thoroughly enjoyed mentoring you. But, that song for me was a little bit dangerous because it's so current right now as Rihanna's record that you have to completely make it like it was never, ever written for her, and I don't know if it quite worked for me, but I don't think it makes a difference. I hope to see you in the final."

"Someone's being tactical!" said Cowell, referring to Cole's words. He then put in perspective the band's plight. Noting the huge increase in their stature, he felt moved to remind the viewers that the band would still need public votes. "I've got to tell you guys, I know this is going to sound a bit biased but I thought this song was absolutely perfect for you because it is exactly what I liked about them—they didn't take the safe option. They chose something completely different—they had the guts to do it. Can I just say, you hear all the applause, and people at home might think you're safe, but nobody is safe in this competition and I would urge anyone, please, if they want to see these boys in the final, please pick up the phone and vote for them because they deserve it."

Their next song of the night was "Chasing Cars," by Snow Patrol. It's yearning, emotional melody was the perfect vehicle to attract votes. Who, one wondered, could resist voting for this band as they sang this moving hit? In the feedback, Walsh, as eager as ever to claim a part in the band's family, said, "Liam, Zayn, Niall, Harry, and Louis—I know your names! If there's any justice, all the young kids will pick up their phones and they're going to vote One Direction—you deserve it!" Minogue added, "Guys, you've got through a really tough week and that was such a classy, classy performance! You've just grown up in front of our eyes." Cole said, "This week I was so impressed, you didn't have Zayn, Simon wasn't around, you showed a real level of maturity, and you really deserve a place in the final."

Cowell said, "Guys, Tim, who's been working with you all week, told me that you made a decision this morning to get in at eight in the morning so you could give yourselves more rehearsal time, and that's what it's all about. It's not about excuses, it's about having that great work ethic, picking yourselves up after what was a very tough week, and I said this before—I genuinely mean this—I am proud of you as people as much as artists. That was a great performance—good for you." Good for them—to their immense delight, the public vote sent them through to the following weekend's final. Along with Matt Cardle, Cher Lloyd, and Rebecca Ferguson, they would battle it out to be crowned *X Factor* champion. Was a band about to win the show for the first time?

However, behind the smiles, glitz, and excitement, there was a family tragedy haunting Zayn. His grandfather, described by Zayn as a happy, jovial, and entertaining character, had died during the week. Zayn had traveled home to Bradford to be with his loved ones as they came to terms with the shock and grief of their loss. The fact that Zayn had returned to London to sing on the live show had impressed a lot of those involved with the season—especially Cowell. Zayn's fellow band members supported him as he mourned—they even accompanied him when he traveled home for the funeral. Zayn truly appreciated this loving gesture.

Popularity, unity, and form—as far as the contest

itself went, everything was coming together at just the right time for One Direction.

The Final

The band's prospects seemed strong going into the final. The hysteria of their fan base was deafening, and the band had followed the golden rule of *X Factor* success—to peak later rather than earlier. Among those who were picking them to win were former *X Factor* champions Joe McElderry—the Geordie singer whose success had spurred several members of One Direction to enter the show—and Alexandra Burke. However, a poll published in the *Sun* newspaper on the morning of the final had them as a distant third behind Rebecca Ferguson and the poll's predicted winner, Matt Cardle.

In the week before the big showdown, the remaining finalists made the customary journeys to their respective hometowns. These always made for compelling and emotional television—they also serve to galvanize the "home" support for each act. Though, due to snow, the band did not travel to

Niall's Ireland. They visited the hometowns of the other members, including Liam's Wolverhampton, where they performed in front of five thousand people. Liam said the experience was "absolutely awesome—the crowd were absolutely amazing." He was also amazed that the frenzy was so intense that police were needed to hold the fans back. The band was "buzzing," he remembered later. Harry added that it was "really exciting for us to think we're going to be doing loads of little gigs like that and some to bigger crowds than that."

On the big night, the band tried to put the newspaper poll out of their minds and focus on the task at hand. The final would take place over two nights, with performances and public voting spread over both nights. The first song they sang was "Your Song," by Elton John. With their rival contestants singing less widely known songs, the band hoped that this classic, popular choice would shore up their vote. For this song, Liam got his personal moment in the limelight—for the first verse of the song he stood alone on the dark stage, lit only by a single light. It was the culmination of a personal journey for him—from his 2008 *X Factor* experience, which ended in rejection at the judges' houses phase, to now, standing almost as a solo artist on the stage of the *X Factor* final.

By the end of the first chorus, the band had united behind a row of microphones, with Harry taking the central one. With snowfall, bright white lighting, and a choir of white-clothed singers joining them for the finale of the song, the producers had thrown nearly every *X Factor* cliché at the performance. Walsh was as impressed as ever, "Hey, One Direction, you're in the final—I hope you're here tomorrow night," he said. "It's amazing how five guys have gelled so well. I know you're all best friends. I've never seen a band cause so much hysteria so early in their career. I definitely think that you've got an amazing future. Niall, everybody in Ireland must vote for Niall, yes!"

Minogue echoed Walsh's wish. "Guys, you have worked so hard in this competition. You were thrown together, you deserve to be here and I'd love to see you in the final tomorrow," she said. Cowell said that the first two performances by Cardle and Ferguson were "so good" that his "heart was sinking" over his band's potential for the night. However, he said, the band "gave it 1,000 percent," and added, "it's been an absolute pleasure working with you." He finished by saying, "I really hope people bother to pick up the phone, put you through to tomorrow because you deserve to be there."

The intensity of the evening was almost unbearable. One thing no critic could take away from the show is that it knows how to perfectly build the tension of the final weekend. The excitement soared anew when the finalists performed their duets. Cardle sang with Rihanna, Lloyd with Will.i.am of the Black Eyed Peas, and Ferguson with Christina Aguilera—all highly prestigious artists. However, One Direction felt that they had the best of all—Robbie Williams. The man who had influenced them so much was about to join them to sing on primetime television.

Their faces radiated with excitement, pride, and almost disbelief as he joined them during their rendition of "She's the One." Each of the boys looked so happy it was impossible for viewers' hearts not to melt. Even Zayn smiled. The fact that the performance went so smoothly was a relief to all. When Williams had sung with a previous finalist, Olly Murs, he had missed his cue, ruining what should have been one of that final's key moments of drama. Williams had also endured a mishap on the show earlier in that season, when the doors failed to open on time for his dramatic stage entrance to sing his comeback single "Bodies," making his eventual appearance somewhat frenzied.

As his successful duet with One Direction came to an end, he shouted, "The lads—One Direction! Phone-in!" and then all six disappeared briefly into a group hug. Robbie even lifted Niall into the air. Louis said he was, "An absolutely massive Robbie fan—thank you so much for doing this with us." To which Robbie casually replied, "Oh it's a pleasure— you guys rock!" Harry, looking more serious than ever, spoke of the "pleasure it had been to sing with Robbie." Cowell described Robbie as "a great friend to the show—very, very generous with his time and he's made [tonight] these boys' night of their lives." The excitement was enough to send the band through the first public vote of the weekend. It was Cher Lloyd who was sent home, leaving One Direction to battle it out with Cardle and Ferguson the following evening.

On Sunday, the stakes were as high as ever. In what would be their final performance of the season, One Direction sang "Torn." As the song they had sung at judges' houses, this was an emotional choice. It reminded the boys themselves—as well as the audience—of how far they had come. Their opponents, Cardle and Ferguson, sang Katy Perry's "Firework" and Eurythmics' "Sweet Dreams," respectively. The next count of the votes would eliminate one of the three, leaving the final two to battle it out.

The final judges' verdicts for the band were all upbeat, but were, for the most part, phrased in expectation that this was the end of the road in the competition. "You've got brilliant chemistry, I love the harmonies. I love the song choice and we've got five new pop stars!" Walsh told them. Minogue added, "Guys, you've done all the right things to make your place here in the final. That was a fantastic performance. Whatever happens tonight, I'm sure you guys are going to go on and release records and be the next big band." Cole added, "It's been so lovely to watch you guys from your first audition. To think that was only a few months ago! I really believe that you've got a massive future ahead of you and I wanna say 'thank you' for being such lovely guys to be around." Only Simon Cowell, predictably, spoke of the band surviving the next cut and winning the show. "Let's be clear—anyone who comes into this final has got a great chance of bettering their future," he said. "But this is a competition and in terms of the competition, in terms of who's worked the hardest, who I think deserves to win based on the future of something we haven't seen before. I would love to hear your names read out at the end of the competition—because I think you deserve it."

With Cher Lloyd already gone, the weekend had thus far conformed to the prediction in the *Sun* poll. If that conformity continued, then One Direction would leave the show at this stage. With Matt Cardle and Dannii Minogue on the left of the stage and Rebecca Ferguson and Cheryl Cole on the right, the One Direction boys were in the middle, standing with Simon Cowell. Complete with the customary, agonizing dramatic pauses, Dermot O'Leary announced that first Cardle and then Ferguson were through, which left One Direction out of the remainder of the contest.

Cowell was the first to react to the disappointing news. He looked distraught, almost angry, as he turned his back on the cameras. It was the body language of disgust. The boys looked absolutely devastated. As one Tweeter commented, "It is like looking through a kaleidoscope at a distraught Justin Bieber."

Louis, befittingly, as the band's oldest member, was the first to speak following this crushing blow. "It's been absolutely incredible," he said. "For me, the highlight was when we first sang together at the judges' houses. That was unbelievable. And you know what? We've done our absolute best, we've worked hard." Zayn, looking to the future, added a defiant note. "We're definitely going to stay together, this isn't the last of One Direction!" he said, to the absolute joy of their fans across the country, whose hearts had sunk when the boys' exit was confirmed.

The show, though, had to go on without One Direction, who watched from the wings. When Cardle was named the winner, the boys were delighted for him. As he sang his winners' song, "When We Collide," the other finalists ran to join him on the stage. The celebratory mob that ensues at this point is always a moving part of the final—it has been a tradition since the final of the first season of *Pop Idol* in 2002. The members of One Direction were as lively as anyone during the massive huddle around Cardle. The ever-bubbly Niall was first out of the throng to embrace the winner, who looked stunned, but delighted.

As Cardle was swallowed up by the mob, Harry sang the lyrics back to him while Niall moved to the front of the stage to amp up the audience into more frenzied cheering and singing. It really was the best moment of the show.

Looking back over the season in an interview with *Digital Spy*, Harry recounted, "When we walked in and saw the studio for the first time; then when us five stood behind the doors for the first time on the live show, for that first song—for me, that was the best moment. That was where we were actually doing it, the real thing, for the first time. That was a big moment." Would they have believed, at that moment in week one, that they would make it all the way to the final? Though their disappointment at not winning the show was huge, it was matched by the pride they had for doing so well in the competition.

Their pride was well deserved. There was just one small, but ever so important, question in their minds. What next?

8 WHAT MAKES THEM BEAUTIFUL

After they were eliminated, the band was called to a private meeting with Cowell. "I've made a decision," he told them, then embarked on a dramatic pause— it must have felt like they were back on-air! Finally, he told them what that decision was: He was going to sign them to his division of Sony Records. Good old "Uncle Simon" had shown that, even when the cameras are not focused on him, he cannot resist leaving people hanging on his words.

For the band, this was the news they had longed to hear. Though many commentators had speculated that Cowell would sign the band whether they won the contest or not, none of the boys had taken that for granted. They knew that the entertainment industry is a ruthless one in which tough decisions are made regardless of the feelings of the people involved. As they heard the news, their emotions were so strong that Harry burst into tears—his cool persona entirely forgotten in the midst of the moment. They could not wait to tell their parents. Like many performers, the boys are eager to make their parents proud.

Cowell told the band, "You have to enjoy yourselves. You're going to make a lot of money, but you have to enjoy every single minute of it." Though the guys did not realize this right away, Cowell had almost made a noteworthy sacrifice. He felt that he had such a promising prospect on his hands that he invited other divisions of Sony to make offers to him before he decided where to send the boys. Rather than automatically signing them to his division, he was willing to consider handing them elsewhere. He explained why to *Rolling Stone*. "This was such an important signing, we let three or four of the Sony labels make a presentation," he said. "I didn't automatically give it to my own label. I thought, 'This is so important, if somebody can come up with a better idea . . .' I was actually willing to pass them along to another division of Sony because I thought the group were that important."

Triumphant, the band then went their separate ways for Christmas. Though they were given less than a week off for the festive season, they were just glad to be home with their loved ones—a haven of familiar serenity during a frantic and unfamiliar time. As they celebrated with their families, the boys could take a considered look at how much their lives had changed over the past year.

They were also getting a crash course in the realities of fame. While out shopping over the Christmas break, Zayn had brought a shopping center to a virtual standstill within a minute or two of being recognized. Harry, meanwhile, noted an almost perpetual gathering of fans near his family home. This was his first encounter with such intrusive fandom—and he found himself worrying about them catching a cold.

Around the same time, Louis heard that some fellow Doncastrians were heard scowling that he was unworthy of the fame and success he had achieved. This is typical of the provincial sniping that people in the spotlight sometimes face. It should be seen for what it is—envy. At the time, though, it was hard to take, particularly for one as young as Louis. Just weeks earlier, Louis had faced similar comments from former *X Factor* winner Steve Brookstein. The middle-aged crooner, who has taken his own fall from fame notoriously badly, wrote on Twitter that Louis was the "luckiest man in music" for landing a record deal. Steve was about to become one of the first people to encounter the full wrath of the One Direction fans.

As the fans raged at Brookstein on Twitter, Louis' mother Johanna sent him a pointed message herself. "Hi, I'm Louis's mom," she wrote. "My family have always liked you and bought your records. Why be so cruel? Why shame him in public? He was sad about his audition. He was incredibly nervous. Listen to his YouTube. He is eighteen Steve! I honestly thought you were a nice bloke. Sadly for us now what we were told about you seems accurate." Brookstein was unrepentant, replying: "If you are Louis's mum, get the poor lad some singing lessons for Christmas. A couple of dozen at least." As Twitter neared meltdown due to the sheer weight of Tweets being fired by the fans, Brookstein remained unfazed. 'Listen, he is a rogue trader," he wrote. "A Mickey Mouse cowboy builder. Don't blame me for exposing his poor workmanship. End of." Louis responded with dignity, telling Brookstein, "Steve you're my idol!" It was a classy response to taunting delivered by a man old enough to be his father.

With their welcome, yet all too brief, and Christmas break over, One Direction reunited in London. Their first significant professional task for 2011 was not the hardest one. As mere mortals crunched through cold mornings to get to school, college, or work, One Direction escaped the harsh British winter by flying to the warmer climes of the West Coast of America. They spent five days in Los Angeles—the self-declared capital of the entertainment industry. There, the sun was shining and the city was glittering with stars. The time was spent in a combination of work—including a recording session in a studio and a meeting with leading producer Max Martin—sightseeing and shopping.

On their return to Britain at the end of January, the band had their most extreme encounter with their fans to date, as they were confronted with hundreds of screaming fans when they arrived at Heathrow Airport. Security staff had to grab the band and escort them at great speed to a police van, just to avoid being mobbed by the fans. It was a crazy experience and the band members responded in different ways. Louis, for example, "got a real buzz" from it, but Niall was completely freaked out.

Former Boyzone lead singer, Ronan Keating, a heartthrob himself back in the 1990s, arrived at the airport around the same time as One Direction. Once upon a time, he had faced scenes such as this. He wrote on Twitter, "Just landed at Heathrow and when I walked out there were hundreds of screaming fans sadly not for me HaHa. One Direction were on flight." Still, the experience brought back fond memories for Keating.

Next on the agenda for the band was their part in *The X Factor* tour, where even more screaming girls would be present to threaten their eardrums. Joining most of the other finalists from the series, they performed in arenas across the country to the show's most dedicated fans. They were put through their paces in the days before the tour—they had to learn new dance moves and also prepare some for between the songs. The rehearsals were serious— they went over some parts of their performances over twenty times. These were tough days, but the effort was well worth it.

On the tour, they shared a dressing room with the other male artists. They were reunited with Matt Cardle, Aidan Grimshaw, and even the comical Wagner. It made for a crowded and energy-filled room as they laughed, remembering the funny times during the series, and also looked to their respective futures. After each show, they would head to their hotel, often partying the rest of the night away. On two separate occasions, they ended up having "fruit fights." The first, in Sheffield, England, lasted for five anarchic minutes. It kicked off when Louis casually tried to launch an apple core into the trash. There was a second fruit fight in Liverpool. No wonder Harry said that he never wanted the tour to end. Vegetables also played a comical part in the tour. After Louis had jokingly commented in an interview that he likes girls who eat carrots, they were bombarded with carrots by the fans. Girls would arrive at their shows and appearances waving banners featuring carrots, wearing carrot T-shirts, and carrying handfuls of them. During one of the concerts, Louis took to the stage wearing a carrot costume. As Louis later joked, all these carrots around him meant he was now able to "see in the dark!"

They loved every moment on stage. From the opening night in Birmingham, England—when the deafening noise from the 12,000-strong crowd that greeted them blew the boys away—through the other cities, including the ones in Ireland, it was a time they would never forget. It also served as a useful apprenticeship for the touring experience. In the future, they would fill venues just as large—and even larger—than those on the *X Factor* tour. Generally, successful bands slowly build their live career from small venues to medium-sized and then to the biggies, rather than selling out massive arenas on their first tour. So it was a big help that the boys had already had the experience of being on stage in front of such huge crowds.

Their key memories of the tour include the several occasions that Liam's pants ripped onstage. It was always during their rendition of "Forever Young" that his "wardrobe malfunctions" occurred. Safe to say, none of the girls in the audience were about to ask for their money back! At the wrap party, which was held in a hotel nightclub after the final performance, the crew, management, and artists fondly bid farewell to the tour and each other. The tour had established that the biggest party animals of the band were Harry and Louis, with most witnesses agreeing that Louis probably beat out Harry for the championship.

In a foreshadowing of the hectic schedule that awaited them, the band were involved with other projects during the tour. The most significant one was the filming of a television commercial for the Nintendo DS Pokemon product. This ad was hardly strenuous work for the band. It was shot in a hotel room and essentially featured them goofing around. They were each given a free DS Pokemon as part of the deal. Another promotional project they were involved with at this time was the release of their first official book, *Forever Young*. Frenzied signing appearances helped push sales of the title ever higher—it ended up quite a hit in the bestseller charts. With other books published about the band in the months after the series, One Direction were in a strange position—they were a pop band with more books than records to their names. This was about to change.

With the tour over, the band took some time off. Niall headed to Spain with his father and a friend; Liam went to Florida with his parents; Louis and Harry went skiing in Courchevel in the French Alps.

On their return, they were ushered into the studio to record their debut single. The song that had been carefully chosen for them was "What Makes You Beautiful." It begins with a brief, staccato guitar riff, with an up-tempo feel to it, reminiscent of the early material of McFly. Then the sound of a drumstick on a cymbal ushers in the first verse. Liam's voice is heard first. In deep tones, he delivers the attention-grabbing opening line. The back-up becomes richer for the bridge, sung by Harry. His soulful, dreamy voice is at its best as he leads the track to its explosive chorus. At which point the full, anthemic quality of the song becomes clear.

In verse two, the song takes a slight detour in style. Zayn's delivery takes in a degree of rap and gives the song a touch—though only a light touch—of "edge." Harry's bridge then takes us back to the chorus. Following which, that classic pop trick of a "na na-na na" chant is deployed until the *a capella* begins, which Harry sings. It is an unexpected moment of quiet and calm—all the better to precede the final chorus, which crashes in supremely. Both in the video and in live performances, the band excites the audience during the chorus. It is not a song that should end with a fade—and it doesn't. Instead, a final "That's what makes you beautiful" from Harry closes the three minutes and eighteen seconds of pop perfection.

It was a well selected song for the band, setting them apart from British boy bands of recent times, avoiding the ballad-heavy, key-change trend. Instead, "What Makes You Beautiful" played to the strength of the members of One Direction—it was mischievous, young, flippant, profound, and uplifting. Never had a generation of girls been more inclined to flip their hair.

Written by Rami Yacoub, Carl Falk, and Savan Kotecha, who between them have written for Westlife, Britney Spears, Nicki Minaj, Usher, and Celine Dion, it was, in truth, pretty much teen pop gold. Musically, its chord progression is bright and its production, masterminded by Yacoub and Falk, soundly simplistic. Praise must go to those behind the track as well to those who selected it for One Direction—songs such as this, which so perfectly both capture and define the spirit of teenage pop, might sound easy to produce, but they aren't.

The boys understood all this only too well. "When we were recording in the studio we knew instantly that we wanted this track to be our first single," Harry told Digital Spy, adding, "I think for us, we wanted to release something that wasn't cheesy but it was fun. It kind of represented us; I think it took us a while to find it but I think we found the right song." Liam, too, felt it was right up their alley. "We always wanted [the debut single] to be something that people didn't expect and then when we heard it, it wasn't what we expected either, so it kind of fitted perfectly." The release was surrounded by pressure, too, something the boys were more than used to. "There's a lot of expectation," said Louis. "All the fans know we've been busy recording, so there's a bit of pressure."

The sound was attributed to a wide range of influences. As well as the aforementioned McFly, they also claimed nods at the style of artists as diverse as American pop giants 'N Sync, 1970s prog-rock dinosaurs Pink Floyd, and the Mexican pop-folk classic "La Bamba." Many also noted a connection between the opening riff and that of the *Grease* song, "Summer Loving." There was a pleasant serendipity here, as some of the boys had appeared in school productions of that very musical.

On its release, on September 11, 2011, the critics were thrilled. Summing up the theme of the song as one that showed that the band's favorite type of girl is, "That endangered breed who are visually stunning but aren't aware of it," online entertainment website Digital Spy's Robert Copsey heaped praise on the track. Giving it four out of five stars, he declared it a cross between Pink and McFly, concluding, "Like a Forever Friends bear from your high school crush, it's adorable, completely innocent, and bound to cause a stir." As a website that lives for reality television and its graduates, Digital Spy could be expected to look on the song favorably. A less expected champion of the song was the New Musical Express (*NME*), in which Ailbhe Malone declared it as "so unthreatening it might have to think twice about holding hands, lest it get overwhelmed." However, she said this was not "a bad thing."

Taking an unsurprisingly technical musical look at the song, Malone continued, "Channeling their sterling performance of 'My Life Would Suck Without You,' 'What Makes You Beautiful' is exuberant with a catchy 'oh na na na' middle eight. The real genius is that the chord progression is simple enough to be played on an acoustic guitar at a house party." The children's TV *Newsround* website gave the single four stars out of five, saying, "Think summer, think sunshine, think parties on the beach, and you'll get the general vibe of 'What Makes You Beautiful'. It's classic pop—fun, upbeat and incredibly catchy." As we shall see, it was not just the critics, nor the record-buying public, that loved the song—so too did award academies.

First, though, let us take a look at its commercial performance, something the band could hardly wait to see. "I'm excited because it's what I've been working toward all my life and it's finally happening," Zayn told *Top of the Pops* magazine, before the single's release. By the time it was released, such a juggernaut of expectation had been created for it, that there was no doubt it would be a big hit. Three weeks ahead of the release date, Sony Music announced that the single had already broken all records for the numbers of pre-orders for a label in the company's history—quite an achievement when you consider that Sony is the home of international superstars including Michael Jackson, Beyoncé, and Christina Aguilera. On release, the song debuted at number one in Britain and Ireland. In due course it would perform very well in other territories, too.

The promotional video for the song is, of course, a considerable part of its success. This part of any band's image has been important since the dawn of MTV in the 1980s. However, in the modern Internet age, the video's importance has assumed a new dimension—thanks to YouTube and social networking sites, management can, to an extent, bypass the mainstream media and market their videos directly to the fans. One Direction had filmed their single's video over two days in July, in Malibu, California. Directed by director, cinematographer, and photographer John Urbano, in it they are seen frolicking on the beach, driving an RV, playing with a soccer ball, and much more. Their fun is infectious. As he delivers the line about flipping hair in the first chorus, Harry flips his own much-loved curly mane.

A group of young ladies join the fun a minute or so in, but it's when the band take their tops off to play in the ocean that the interest of most viewers will increase. The fact that there are but a few brief scenes of their topless torsos was deliberate. This was less a tease and more a determination on the part of the band's management to not overly sexualize them at this early stage of their career. Noting, for example, the way that Justin Bieber had first conquered the world of pop with a basically squeaky-clean and wholesome image, the management were determined that One Direction should not leap out of their clothes at the first moment as other boy bands had done.

The most intimate moment of the video comes when Harry sings the *a capella* part up close and personal to one of the female models. It is, in truth, a slightly awkward moment. Harry looks fairly—but not entirely—comfortable. The actress, though, seems far less at home and, the fans will have noted with passion, not entirely thrilled to be in such a scene. The shoots for pop videos can be lengthy and tiring experiences, so hopefully the fans—who would have killed to have been in her shoes that day—can forgive her.

Meanwhile, the band had more promotional appearances to fulfill. Their first major television interview appearance was on *Alan Carr: Chatty Man*. With the help of Carr's considerable wit and outrageous chatter, the band's personalities came across well. They managed to dispel the suspicion held by some members of the public that boy band members are vapid and dull characters. Instead, they had the audience in stitches. Harry in particular was oozing charisma.

Some highlights of the band's appearance on the show included Niall's amazingly convincing imitation of *X Factor* announcer Peter Dickson's voice, and Louis' funny tales of American car mishaps. Carr also asked Louis about Brookstein's online attack on him. "Does your mum always come and defend you?" asked the host. Louis, to everyone's amusement, had to admit that she did.

The band also performed their single on the Cowell-created game show *Red or Black*. This appearance turned out to be a less happy experience. For part of the song the audience were shown a specially acted video of the band traveling to the television studio via the subway underground, singing the first two versus and choruses on the train among the fans, and then being chased from the underground station, down the road to the TV studio by screaming fans. What was meant as a simple fun gimmick was instead interpreted by some viewers as evidence that the band were being shielded from giving a full performance due to a lack of talent when it came to live performances.

One would have thought that seeing Harry clearly sing the *a capella* section live onstage should have been enough to dispel those thoughts. His nerves—and breathlessness having danced around on-stage—were both clear. His hands shook as he sang and his eyes looked more than a little anxious. When he completed the solo part successfully, he breathed a sigh of relief, Niall patted him on the shoulder, and the band launched back into the full crashing chorus. It had all been all right—or had it?

When they came off air, Harry said he "felt a little sorry for himself" over the way he had let his nerves show. He logged onto Twitter and searched to see what was being said about him online. He was devastated by the extent of the abuse that he found.

Louis tried to comfort him but realized there was not much he could do. "I felt powerless," said Louis later.

The band rallied round Harry and assured him that they and the fans still adored him. For many fans, Harry's nerves had only made him seem more real and adorable. It reminded the fans that this was a new band comprised of young men. One Direction were on the way to becoming the top dogs of British pop but they retained the image of the underdog. They were being styled and managed well. Since they left *The X Factor,* they had been physically transformed only to an extent—they looked and behaved more like pop stars but were still recognizable as the boys who had appeared for their first auditions. Next up for One Direction was the ultimate moment.

Called *Up All Night,* One Direction's debut album was a carefully selected, brilliantly produced piece of work. It begins with the aforementioned "What Makes You Beautiful." In an album with several surprises and changes of pace, the first occurs with track two—in contrast to the opener, "It's Gotta Be You" is a classic boy band ballad. Here, the lyrics are full of regret for hurt that has been unintentionally caused. Who cannot relate to the wish that time could be rewound? Gorgeous strings turn this into an epic affair that delights the listener—it is no wonder it was chosen as a subsequent single.

Track three is essentially a return to the impish, pop-rock atmosphere of the opener. "One Thing" is the natural sibling to "What Makes You Beautiful." In many ways, the lyrics mirror their own story—when they sing, they need that one thing, the one thing the girl in the song has. They also could be singing of themselves, because they have that indefinable one thing that Simon Cowell and the music industry itself needed. "More Than This," the slowest and most gentle track on the album, features some astonishing falsetto vocals, which show the range of the band. The song is also notable for a fine solo from Louis, whose performance is a fair response to the online sniping that occurred in the previous year.

Track five is the album's title tune, "Up All Night," and is a vivid call to arms to the party generation. "I Wish" is a mid-tempo sound, very much in the "album track" mode—there is nothing wrong with it, but it does not leap out at the listener, while "Tell

Me a Lie" is a song that would be prefect to listen to while driving on the highway. Its successor, "Taken," is, in contrast, one to be sung around a bonfire, complete with acoustic guitars. Harry has arguably never sounded better than he does on this track in which the boys are defiant rather than doting "Who do you think you are?" they ask, a hint of menace in their voices.

If the next song, "I Want," reminds the listener of a mid-career track by McFly, that is for good reason because it was written by their chief songwriter, Tom Fletcher. Despite making some unflattering remarks about One Direction when they first came to the public eye, Fletcher quickly noted their commercial potential and happily handed them this song. "Everything About You" is far more electro and mainstream pop in sound. Some strong lyrics lift it out of the pack, again underscoring the attention that has gone into the entire album.

"Same Mistakes" is a sweet, rolling ballad, the rich backing track smoothly enhancing the vocals. With the penultimate track, the band say they want to save a girl from her current lot in life. As such, "Save You Tonight," a song that could easily be performed by JLS or The Wanted, pushes multiple buttons. Few fans would resist such salvation from these boys. For a moment, when the final track kicks in, the listener's ear is tricked into wondering if it is a cover of Taio Cruz's "Dynamite." Then, during the bridge, the song momentarily sounds like Rihanna's "Only Girl (in the World)." An impressive anthem ending an impressive album.

To bring the album to fruition, the band had worked with a string of big names—Wayne Hector, the man who wrote Westlife's mega hit "Flying Without Wings," being one of them. Another was Steve Robson, who had worked with James Morrison and Busted. The two people they worked with who excited them the most were RedOne, who has co-produced a string of hits for Lady Gaga, and Ed Sheeran, the ginger-haired singer-songwriter sensation.

"Getting to write and record with Ed Sheeran on our album was an honor," said Niall. Harry agreed, commenting that the people they worked with on the album were "legendary." Liam, meanwhile, was delighted to work with "hit machine" Claude Kelly, the man behind "Grenade." They recorded it in both the U.K. and America, and in total, there were twenty-two songwriters involved in the tracks. On top of this, the band members themselves get co-writing credits on three of the songs.

The album debuted at number two in the U.K. charts. Impressive in itself—and things became still more impressive when it became the fastest-selling debut album on the U.K. Albums Chart of 2011. It also reached the top 10 in other countries including Sweden, Ireland, Netherlands, New Zealand, and Australia. (It was set for release in America in March 2012.) The *Sun*'s face of showbiz Gordon Smart declared, "*Up All Night* will be lapped up by their young fan-base" and praised it for its blend of sounds and styles. *Cosmopolitan* magazine felt that the album was full of "toe-tappers that are just impossible to dislike;" the *Independent* newspaper said the album would "sell by the zillion;" while the *Daily Star* said it was full of "belting fun pop anthems."

In the wake of the album's release, One Direction took to the road on their first headline tour. Beginning in the middle of December in Watford, England, they played in cities across the U.K. and

Ireland in shows that had sold out within minutes of them going on sale. As well as singing tracks from their album and the B-side "Na, Na, Na," they also performed some covers. Among these were "I Gotta Feeling," by Black Eyed Peas, The Zutons/Amy Winehouse track "Valerie," and "Use Somebody" by Kings of Leon. There were also "snowball" fights with the plastic snowballs that fell from above, followed later by silver streamers. With Niall plucking on his acoustic guitar for parts of the set, and the band indulging in much between-track banter, the shows were loads of fun. Naturally, the other ingredient of the experience was the screams of the fans lucky enough to get tickets. Even seasoned concert goers and staff at the venues were taken aback by the volume of the noise. The only downside of the tour came when a car smashed into their tour bus in early January. Although three of the band who were inside the bus at the time suffered head and neck pains, as well as shock, there were no serious injuries.

9 THE AMERICAN DREAM

Formed in 2010 and releasing a single and an album in 2011, One Direction wanted to up their game in 2012. The year of 2012 has long been predicted by some to augur the end of the world, but One Direction wanted it to be the start of a whole new life for them. The prospect of becoming a one-minute wonder who would disappear as fast as they had appeared, haunted each member of the band. They wanted to be in the music industry for the long haul and to make their success truly global. They were not even content to merely replicate the fun and success of 2011—they wanted to soar over and better it. Ahead of them were several significant opportunities to do just that. Starting with a trip to Britain's most prestigious music awards night, The BRITs.

Held at the O2 Arena in February, the BRIT Awards 2012 was hosted by Louis' old pal James Corden. It turned out to be an evening of highs and lows for the band. One of the lows would haunt them for months. First, though, came the high. They were nominated in the Best British Single category. Given how many successful bands never win a BRIT during their career, the fact that One Direction was already on the brink of winning their first was flushed with significance. For their category, a public vote had been held to decide the winner. It was listeners to the British Capital FM radio station who had voted, but in the excitement of winning the award, Harry thanked the listeners of Capital's rival Radio One by accident.

Their excitement as they were named winners was palpable. Onstage to present the award to them was pop star Tinie Tempah. "Wow," said Louis. "We cannot believe that we are here." He then added that, "this award is for the fans." Harry was next to speak. After echoing Louis' thanks to the fans, he added, "And a massive thank you to Radio One." Mindful of the enormous damage this could cause One Direction's chances of air-time on Capital, the

Starting out with a bang, their debut single "What Makes You Beautiful" tops the U.K. charts.

Above: Despite becoming an overnight success, boys will still be boys.

Below: The band launches *Up All Night*—the fastest-selling album of 2011.

The only way is up: One Direction on the Up All Night tour that began in December 2011 and performed in Europe, Australasia, and North America.

Left: At the BRIT Awards 2012: the boys chat with host James Corden.

Below: Fun-loving Niall jokes around.

Right: Ecstatic as they cradle their award for Best British Single.

Conquering the States: One Direction became the first British group to reach number one on the U.S. *Billboard* chart with their debut album. (*Above*) Performing at the Nickelodeon 25th Annual Kids' Choice Awards. (*Below*) Being interviewed on the radio in New York.

Right: The band heads Down Under where Liam enjoys the surf.

Left: Who's the cutie? Louis hugs a koala.

Chilling out in the sunshine, the boys enjoy a well-earned break.

From talent-show contestants to global stars—there's only One Direction.

band's PR firm issued a swift statement via Twitter. "One Direction forgot to thank the Capital Radio listeners last night when picking up their BRIT Award for 'Best British Single'," read the statement. "This was an oversight as the boys were caught up in the excitement of winning. The band would like to take this opportunity to thank Capital Radio and all their listeners for their support and for voting for them."

Although Harry was kicking himself over his slip-up, he and his band mates tried hard to not let it get in the way of some serious celebration. During an interview, they were asked how they would divide the single trophy between them; they joked that they would either cut it into pieces or photocopy it.

During his part of their acceptance speech, Liam had mentioned that they were about to announce an arena tour. The band did just that, unveiling a string of dates, beginning at London's O2 Arena on February 22, 2013. The fifteen dates sold out within a few minutes of going on sale. A list of twenty new shows was quickly added, including matinée performances in London, Cardiff, Manchester, and Birmingham. The speed in which they sold out Britain's biggest arenas was incredible—One Direction were, by this measure, the kings of the U.K. pop scene.

If February 2012 had been fun, then March would be magnificent. They cracked the all important and almost impossible American market. When one looks at the list of top British and Irish artists that have failed to replicate their success overseas, one begins to appreciate the scale of the challenge. Among those who flopped there are Westlife, Robbie Williams, and Oasis. Busted, then Britain's biggest pop band and also huge in Japan, even made an MTV documentary, *America or Busted* that focused on their inability to make it there. With bands who had ruled the British charts for years failing in America, who would have held out hope for One Direction?

However, more or less immediately after they arrived in America for the big push, they found that they had a huge, fanatical, and vocal following. They were mobbed in Boston and, when they moved to Toronto in Canada, the police were called after a crowd so huge and excitable surrounded their hotel. The music industry journal, *Billboard*, said, "There's a lot of possibility here, there's a lot of upside . . . that level of talent with those kinds of looks . . . it's really a perfect storm for a massive, massive successful phenomenon." Given how hard it can be to impress the American media, these were very promising words.

The band were finding that, rather than experiencing the fruitless and soul-destroying slog that many British bands encounter in the U.S., they were already a success. Comparisons were soon being made between the band and Britain's biggest musical export. Not only did One Direction get a spot on the *Today Show*, the biggest morning television show in America, they were mentioned on the show as a band akin to The Beatles. "Now at 8.39 A.M., with the group that some people are saying are inspiring the next case of Beatlemania ..." said the presenter. "Odds are, if you do have a teenager in your house, or a pre-teen girl, she's already obsessed with One Direction." The band duly appeared at the *Today Show* plaza, in the shadow of New York's iconic Rockefeller Center. They also appeared on another landmark U.S. television show, *Saturday Night Live*. Hugely successful and established bands that had never made it onto either show could only watch with envy.

"What Makes You Beautiful" first charted in America at number 28—the highest *Billboard* Hot 100 debut for a U.K. band for fourteen years. As if this wasn't exciting enough, even better news was just around the corner. Just stop for a moment and imagine the joy they felt when they were told that they had become the first U.K. pop group to debut at number one on the U.S. *Billboard* album chart with *Up All Night*. They were stunned and humbled by the news. "We simply cannot believe that we are number one in America," said Harry. "It's beyond a dream come true for us. We want to thank each and every one of our fans in the U.S. who bought our album and we would also like to thank the American public for being so supportive of us." Niall added, "As you can imagine, we are over the moon." Their mentor and adopted uncle, Simon Cowell, was bursting with pride. "I couldn't be happier for One Direction, it is an incredible achievement," he wrote on his Twitter account. "They deserve it. They have the best fans in the world."

This was not only exciting for One Direction and their fans, it was a moment of pride for Britain. They were not the only British boy band making a big splash in America. The Wanted were also proving to be a hit there—their single "Glad You Came" peaked at number 4 on the *Billboard* Hot 100. Even better news came when American fans of One Direction explained that they loved the band not in spite of them being British but because of it. "It just makes them cuter," said one fan.

Later, in his interview with *Rolling Stone* magazine, Simon Cowell put into context how they had pulled off this success story. Speaking of the big bands who had flopped in America, he said, "I think with most of these bands, you end up with a sound that sounds somewhere between England and America—which means you fall smack down in the middle of the ocean. You don't appeal to either." The vehicle that drove the success was, without a doubt, online social networking. Thanks to Twitter, Facebook, and Tumblr, the band was already being marketed in the U.S. by the most enthusiastic team possible—the fans themselves. Justin Bieber's success, which was originally largely due to to YouTube and Twitter, had taught everyone a lesson—teenage artists can bypass the old-fashioned promotional routes. Therefore, Cowell could afford to be optimistic. He noticed, as he launched *The X Factor USA* in 2011, that teenage girls were already taking an interest in the band. They kept asking him when he would bring One Direction to America.

Cowell allowed this frenzy to build organically. "Normally we hassle the American labels when we think something is going to work," he told *Rolling Stone*. "This time we said, 'Let's just wait for the phone to ring and see who phones first.' I wanted them to find out about the group first in a more buzzy way rather than us forcing the band on them."

While Cowell believes that the impact of social networking on the industry is "great news" and that "for the music business, social networking is brilliant," he makes sure to emphasize that an artist or band needs an inherent charm and spark in order to make a success of this very modern method of marketing. "The band has to make it happen by themselves," he said. "I think that's what One Direction did. We worked as a partnership, but without their input and the way they spoke to the fans and the kind of people they are, it wouldn't have happened in the way that it's happening now."

One of Cowell's key employees agrees. "Sometimes

you feel the song's the star, but it's not like that here—it's the act," Sonny Takhar, managing director of Syco, told the *Guardian*. "It's a real moment," added Takhar. "Social media has become the new radio, it's never broken an act globally like this before." How sustainable social media is in this sense remains to be seen. For instance, while Lily Allen and Arctic Monkeys used the MySpace network to great effect in launching their careers, the tsunami of mediocre acts that then flooded MySpace with their own material quickly devalued the forum. As Cowell himself admits, "there's tons of groups out there. It doesn't happen to everyone."

In addition to the factors outlined by Cowell, one should consider that the American market had a yawning gap for a new boy band. Groups like New Kids on the Block, the Backstreet Boys, and 'N Sync had never been truly replaced. Even The Jonas Brothers, who inhabited a slightly different part of the market, had long since peaked. One Direction, and their fellow British boy band The Wanted, came along at just the right time. One Direction's success in America can be explained by a potent combination of charm and timing—they arrived as a new method of marketing was in its prime and when the market itself was craving a band just like them. Some guys get all the luck.

However, not everything went their way in America. Soon after they arrived, news broke that a U.S. band, also called One Direction, were planning to sue over the use of their name by the British band. The U.S. band's lawyer, Peter Ross, claimed to the *Hollywood Reporter* that the band and their management had been made aware for a while of the name-clash issue. "Rather than change their name or do anything to create confusion or avoid damage to our goodwill, they chose to press ahead and come on their tour," Ross said. "We've been in negotiations for a month to find a resolution. In our view, the negotiations weren't turning out to be very productive."

Even as this tangle continued, the band had plenty to console themselves with. Their popularity did not diminish at all as a result of the dispute. If anything, it solidified the support of the fans for the British band. It gave everyone something to unite against. On Twitter and other social networking websites, the almost unanimous response to the battle was one of support for the British band. Asked on Australian television if they would be changing their name, Harry and Zayn both said "no". Zayn then added, "We don't know [what will happen] but we're not changing our name."

Alongside this surge of love and support was the fact that the five boys were making serious money from their success. There has sometimes been a perception that even those who build a successful career from shows like *The X Factor* never make any money. Instead, goes the belief, that the managers make all the money, leaving next to nothing for the artists themselves, who are locked into contracts that are cleverly designed to throw them only scraps. However, the experience of artists as diverse as Leona Lewis and Jedward suggests otherwise. Both apparently have made a great deal of money since their *X Factor* experiences.

In the case of One Direction, reports claimed that as of April 2012, each member had already made over $1.5 million. "Simon Cowell wants them to know what they deserve. They have been a massive success, what they have achieved is phenomenal. Simon thinks they are the hardest-working people in pop at the moment," a source told *People*. In the same month, some statistics emerged to back up that figure. For instance, "What Makes You Beautiful" went platinum in the U.S. after selling 1,129,852 units in the first few months after its release. This was quite remarkable by any standards. Established British bands would struggle to do so well in America. For a band to do that well with their debut was almost unparalleled.

Meanwhile, they were touring Australia and New Zealand. What an experience all this traveling was for the boys, not least Zayn, who had never been abroad until he took part in *The X Factor*. When they appeared on Australian television, hundreds of fans flocked to stand outside the studio and scream their love for the band. "This is mental, it's absolutely incredible and we can't believe it," said Liam when he and his bandmates saw the scenes. The hysteria was shocking and the police had to work hard to maintain order. One fan said she would be willing to be shot by a stun gun to get close to her heartthrobs. "I'll do anything to see them, I'd even get tasered for this," she said. The band made such an impact Down Under that when tickets for their eighteen shows (to be held there in September 2013) went on sale, all 190,000 were instantly snapped-up. Country by country, One Direction was conquering the world.

10   THE PRICE OF FAME

During an interview while in America, Liam had opened up about the price that comes with fame—especially fame acquired at high speed. "It's all happening so fast, it's hard to take it all in," he said. "Sometimes it's only when I'm on my own, that I think about everything and sometimes I think I would quite like to just go home. There's a part of me that occasionally wants to go back to Wolverhampton and just chill out, play the field, be normal again. It's a Catch 22 situation, I guess." Given the media training each band member had undergone, this was a surprisingly candid moment from Liam. His words reflected each band member's awareness that the relentless workload, insatiable scrutiny, and undoubted pressure that they faced as celebrities could sometimes seem too much to take.

Liam, who dates dancer Danielle Peazer, was under no illusion that amid the scrutiny the band faced came almost excruciating attention on their love lives. It was never going to be otherwise, particularly for a band whose appeal was, to a large extent, based on how they look.

It had been this way ever since the band was first formed. Even while their *X Factor* season was still in progress, Zayn was rumored to be dating Geneva Lane, a member of the girl band Belle Amie. The speculation reached a fever pitch when he was spotted kissing her backstage during the final weekend of the season. He was then seen holding hands with Lane, who is three years older than him, as they left the studios. As far as the press was concerned, these photographs proved the rumors to be true. Zayn, though, had news for them. He wrote on Twitter, "Hey fans, just thought I'd let u guys know don't believe the hype we're just friends and that was a friendly kiss."

This rumor was further muddled by the fact that Lane had earlier, seemingly, confirmed on Twitter that there was a relationship between her and Zayn. "We have a thing," she said during a Twitter exchange with a friend. Her connection with Zayn, whatever the extent and nature of it, meant she was targeted by fans who thought she might be a useful "in" for them with the band. She was bombarded with requests to pass messages to the band, including requests that she set up a coveted "follow" on Twitter. "You know, I find it a bit disrespectful that some people on here consider me to be a personal assistant to 1D," she wrote.

Lane was not the only *X Factor* finalist Zayn has been linked to. He was also reported to have dated runner-up Rebecca Ferguson—and this time the rumors were confirmed. "I'm in love and it's a wonderful feeling," said Ferguson during an interview with *Reveal* magazine. "I've never felt like this before. It took a while before we looked at each other in a different light. There was no one particular moment, it just evolved over time. But he made all the running." Several reports had stated that it was Zayn who had been the driving force between the couple getting together. One described him as "very persuasive."

However, the most notorious relationship involving a member of One Direction was, of course,

Harry's relationship with *Xtra Factor* host Caroline Flack. This proved to be a sensational story from the start—the teenage *X Factor* contestant in a relationship with a thirty-something T.V. host. He posted a sign that read, "To Flackster! Never too old . . . Let's make it happen!! Lots of love, Harry S." Reports suggested that they did quickly make it happen—the fling started after he had described her as "gorgeous" and was then seen smooching with her at an after-show party. Flack soon discovered that any woman—particularly an older one—who was linked with a member of the band, would soon face enormous abuse on the Internet. For her, this included being bombarded with death threats every time the media stitched together any details about the romance.

Rebecca Ferguson had already complained about "abuse" from "twelve year olds" during her relationship with Zayn. It seemed that Flack faced an even more fierce backlash, including on Twitter. After feeling sickened by the flood of threats and abuse she was facing, she sent a message out in response. "Hi one direction fans! To clarify. I'm close friends with Harry . . . He's one of the nicest people I know . . . I don't deserve death threats :) x." Reports suggested that Harry's mom was not pleased either and wanted Flack to "keep your hands off my son!"

Given the hectic demands of both parties' careers and the enormous scrutiny they faced as a couple, it was less than shocking when it was revealed that they had split. Harry was said to be the one who called a time-out on the relationship, but, sensitive to the possible damage that being perceived as a "dumper" might cause to his image, he made a rare statement on Twitter, "Please know I didn't 'dump' Caroline. This was a mutual decision. She is one of the kindest, sweetest people I know. Please respect that."

When things had calmed down, Flack finally spoke with more candor about what they had been through. "Harry is adorable, he is a nice person," she told the *Mail on Sunday*. She said that, despite the split, they remained on good terms. "First and foremost we are friends. We got very close for a time, but that's between me and Harry. What happened is between me and him and then we decided it was best to just be friends."

Still, the relationship had become one of the biggest celebrity sagas of recent years and has created a variety of responses. Flack was simultaneously praised and slammed for dating a young man, while Harry faced similar contrary responses. He was soon handed the reputation of a young man who is a passionate admirer of older women. He did little to dispel this perception, when he subsequently hinted he had a thing for thirty-something socialite Kim Kardashian. During an interview in America, he held up a poster of the curvy celebrity; attached to it was a Post-it note on which he had scribbled, "Call me . . . Maybe?" Then, during a television interview, Zayn teased Harry about his crush. "He likes an older woman," said Zayn, much to Harry's discomfort. It was then that Harry stepped in to stop Zayn from going any further. His humor on the issue is wearing thin.

Sadly, the abiding memory from any encounter that a member of One Direction had with a member of the opposite sex was the hassle that came with it for both parties, particularly the woman. The fans' devotion to the band was so intense that a vocal minority of them were willing and—thanks to the online age—able to make life hell for any girl who got close to the band. Liam's girlfriend Danielle had received some unpleasant messages herself. Even Hannah Walker, a pretty blonde who was dating Louis long before he became famous, was ruthlessly targeted on Twitter.

This is a perpetually smoldering issue, but occasionally it ignites into something fiercer. For instance, in April 2012, twenty-year-old Anna Crotti said she had been "bullied" online into canceling a date with Zayn. She had met him during the band's stay in Australia. "A security guard came up to me. I thought I was in trouble but he said, 'The lads want your number,'" she told MTV. "I got a text later saying hello. I asked who it was and it was Zayn." Word soon got out that she was speaking with Zayn, and that was when the trouble started.

"By the end of the day, it got a bit too scary," she said. "Random girls were abusing me on Facebook. Mothers even called me in tears, demanding to know if I knew where One Direction were because their daughters wanted to meet them. I didn't even want to walk home. It was so intense. I messaged Zayn and said, 'Maybe it's not a good idea we meet up.'"

During the same trip, renewed speculation was surrounding Harry's love life. While they were in

New Zealand, he reportedly began dating American model Emma Ostilly. He was said to have taken her on a date and then kissed her on her doorstep. "They really seemed to have a connection and only had eyes for each other," an onlooker was quoted as saying. The suspiciously familiar vocabulary—used in endless quotes from unnamed "sources"—brought the veracity of this into question. After Harry explained that she was "just a friend," Liam backed up his band mate, saying, "She's not his girlfriend either." This was not enough to save her from some fans' venom. She deleted her Twitter account after becoming tired of the hassle.

The band became increasingly frustrated when they saw what the girls they were linked to had to endure. They were in a bizarre position—millions of girls around the world were desperate to fling themselves at them, yet the flipside of that made them strangely difficult young men to date. The band could have been forgiven if they were left wondering whether the "fans" who bombarded their partners with online abuse were really worthy to be described as "fans" at all. Later in April, Louis showed that his patience was wearing thin when he confronted his fans on Twitter. He discovered that, under the hashtag "Louannah"—a nickname used during his relationship with Hannah Walker—fans had been Tweeting his then-girlfriend Eleanor Calder with photographs of him with Walker. He was furious, and took to Twitter to make his feelings known. In an uncharacteristic outburst, he wrote, "Truth of the matter is it's actually not funny in the slightest. I'm reading through some horrible tweets very p*ssed off!" He also sent a message directly to Calder, reassuring her of his feelings, "Love YOU! xxxx" and then added, "I couldn't be happier right now, so let it be :) Thank youuuuu x." He knew his fans would see this message, so it was partially addressed to them, too.

Meanwhile, Hannah Walker, an elementary school teaching assistant who had taken a step back from the limelight since her split with Louis, was dragged back into the fray. She told the *Daily Mail* she was embarrassed by the fuss and that she had taken the trouble to contact Eleanor Calder to tell her it had nothing to do with her. As for her famous ex-boyfriend, she said, "When I look at him on the television now I know him as two different people—

one is the boy from Doncaster, and the other is Louis from One Direction." She just wanted Louis to be happy and it is safe to say that the majority of One Direction fans feel exactly the same way.

It is worth reflecting on the experience of other boy bands to understand how One Direction stand out in regard to their relationships with women. In days gone by, boy band members were often banned by their management from having girlfriends, or at least publicly admitting as much. Take That, for instance, were ordered not to have girlfriends by their management team as it was feared that they would lose appeal to their fans if they were not perceived as being "available" romantically. For One Direction, their team had decided early on to take a different approach. They would be allowed to have girlfriends and to be open about this. At one early meeting with their management, the boys were even encouraged to date slightly older women, as it was felt the "fall out" following any split would be less damaging that way.

"We're trying to do something different from what people would think is the typical kind of boy band," Niall told Canada's *National Post*. "We're trying to do different kinds of music and we're just trying to be ourselves, not squeaky clean." In time, this frenzy that surrounds the girls that any band member is dating may calm; as the real fans, who only wish the boys well, make their voices heard, life will improve for all concerned.

Lest we forget, the One Direction fans are a devoted clan. They have frequently used Twitter to create supportive and kind trends. The band members' frustration over the girlfriend issue was put into perspective by the news that Zayn's aunt had died in February 2012. This happened while the band was in America. A flight was swiftly booked so Zayn could rush home to be with his family. The news was announced by Harry on Twitter, "Zayn has suffered a loss in his family & has had to go home for a few days so won't be at our next shows in the US," wrote Harry. "Our thoughts are with him and his family at this sad time."

The fans were upset to think of their hero suffering—particularly after his grandfather's death during the *X Factor* live shows. They started a hashtag tribute for Zayn and his family, getting the "#StayStrongZayn" to trend on the social network.

215

The first interaction Zayn himself made following his bereavement was to "re-tweet" a message from another user. It read, "God has no Phone, but I talk to him. He has no Facebook, but he is still my friend. He does not have a twitter, but I still follow him. (sic)" That story reflects the real fans of One Direction, who will stick with the band in the future. Having supported them from the very beginning, the fans know that they had—and still have—a part to play in this remarkable story.

So what does the future hold for One Direction? "In the summer, we're going to get back and start a new record," said Niall in March 2012. "We want to bring out a record nearly every year, every year and a half," he added. Preliminary work was already underway for the second album, he said, explaining there had been "meetings and stuff with different writers and producers." Early reports suggest that the band is imagining a heavier sound for album number two. With more than one of the boys being fans of American rock bands like Green Day and Jack's Mannequin, they want to bring some of that vibe to their own material. "We want to take the next album into a different zone—more guitars and grungier," Louis told the *Daily Star*.

It is essential that the ideas, wishes, and thoughts of the band members themselves are always at the center of their development. The guys do not wish to be pop puppets—and their fans wouldn't stand for that. These are five guys with a real creative spark. They are also five decent and kind young men who deserve to be respected. Simon Cowell was once asked how he would make sure that the band sustain their success, rather than fizzing quickly out of favor in the ever-fickle pop industry. His philosophy was simple: "Be sensible and treat them as human beings, genuinely. That's the most important thing."

INDEX

(1D in subentries refers to One Direction)

INDEX

INDEX

BIBLIOGRAPHY

Birth Order, Linda Blair, Piatkus Books, 2011

One Direction A-Z, Sarah Oliver, John Blake Publishing, 2011

One Direction: Dare to Dream: Life as One Direction, One Direction, HarperCollins, 2011

1D: Forever Young, One Direction, HarperCollins, 2011

Simon Cowell: The Unauthorized Biography, Chas Newkey-Burden,
Michael O'Mara Books, 2009

The X Factor: Access All Areas, Jordan Paramor, Headline, 2007

PHOTO CREDITS